Kartar

An Indian Immigrant in East Africa
1927 to 1949

Jaihind S Sumal
Inderpal S Sumal
Kawal Neni Dhillon

PALMETTO
PUBLISHING

Charleston, SC
www.PalmettoPublishing.com

Kartar

Copyright © 2023 by *Jaihind S Sumal, Inderpal S Sumal, Kawal Neni Dhillon*

Hardcover ISBN: 979-8-8229-1050-8
Paperback ISBN: 979-8-8229-1051-5
eBook ISBN: 979-8-8229-1052-2

Dedicated to our Birthplace Kenya and its People

Brothers don't necessarily have to say anything to each other

Table of Contents

Acknowledgments

Part two of the book consists of translations of letters written to Kartar Singh in Kenya, by his two brothers in India. These letters were written in the Arabic-Urdu script but the language was Punjabi. Urdu was introduced to India in the 12th century during the Mughal rule and gradually became the medium of instruction in schools and the main script for government documents and correspondence, especially in Punjab. After India's independence on August 15, 1947, Urdu was phased out and replaced by Punjabi and Hindi scripts.

The authors could not read the Urdu script but were familiar with the Punjabi language used in the letters, which was their mother tongue. A search for someone who could read the script and speak Punjabi led us to Nazir Ahmed Saghir, a dear Kenyan friend of our elder brother Harcharan. The late Saghir was born in Pakistan and migrated to Kenya after marrying the late Bashira Moghal. He was a graduate from Punjab University and later trained as a teacher in Kenya. He had a vast experience of teaching Urdu and Mathematics at Juja Road Primary School and later at Technical High School in Kenya. After migrating to England, he taught at Birmingham University, where in his role as a professor, he helped to facilitate the Urdu and Mathematics skills of his students.

On a request from our brother, Saghir volunteered to record the letters on audio-tapes, a long and tedious task requiring lots of patience to make sense of local words and phrases from faded letters with tattered edges. We are deeply indebted to Saghir, because without his input, the letters would have remained undeciphered.

We are grateful to our father Kartar Singh Sumal for carefully storing these letters and other documents, and for recording his life events on audio tapes and paper. This treasure trove formed the source of the historical and personal accounts in the book. Words cannot express our gratitude to our parents who gave us wings to fly and roots to come back, thus inspiring us to recreate history by bringing to life these long forgotten letters from a bygone era of their youth.

We would like to thank our elder siblings Perminder Kaur Aujla, Harcharan Singh Sumal and our youngest brother Navkiran Singh Sumal for their help in compiling this narrative by providing additional information. We feel blessed to have had our brothers Balbir Singh and Balwinder Singh in our lives, without whom the Sumal family history and legacy would be incomplete.

We are thankful to Kulbir and Khushdev Thind for their help in getting Urdu documents translated to Punjabi.

Special thanks to Pari Dhillon and Ram Dachepalli for their suggestions on improving the contents, and to Dr. Lorna Callaghan for enhancing the book through her painstaking and dedicated editing.

A PAGE FROM AN ORIGINAL HANDWRITTEN LETTER IN URDU,
WRITTEN BY SHANGARA SINGH, DATED 25TH OCTOBER 1947

Sham Singh   Bebeji

Siblings

Wazir Singh   Karam Kaur   Gurmukh Singh   Kartar Kaur   Kartar Singh   Shangara Singh   Gurdial Singh

Spouses

Hukam Singh   Gurbachan Kaur   Sucha Singh   Angrez Kaur   Jaswant Kaur   Gurcharan Kaur

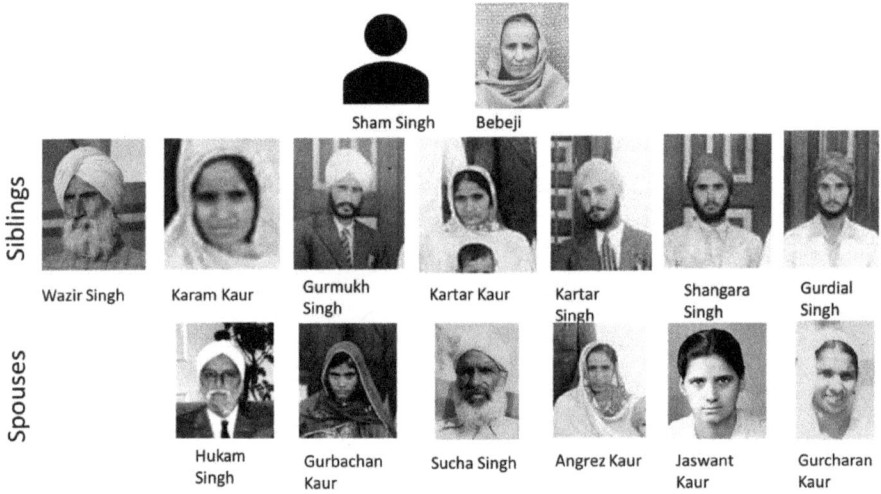

FAMILY TREE — SIKH NAMES END IN 'SINGH' FOR MALES AND IN 'KAUR' FOR FEMALES

Siblings	Wazir Singh	Karam Kaur	Kartar Kaur	Gurmukh Singh	Kartar Singh	Shangara Singh	Gurdial Singh
Spouses		Hukam Singh	Sucha Singh	Gurbachan Kaur	Angrez Kaur	Jaswant Kaur	Gurcharan Kaur
Children (Father: Dial Singh, Mother: Kaseri Arora)		Jeeto Surjit	Bibo Baljeet	Choti Guddi Jasminder	Biri Balbir	Nanhi Kuldip	Jagdev
		Gurmeet	Ballo Jagjit	Walayti Sarmukh	Barhi Guddi Perminder	Lakha Parminder	Guddi Jagdev
		Pali Harpal		Matte Harminder	Chani Harcharan	Guddi Kuldeep	Kakani Baldev
		Bali Baljeet		Ghoge/Bessi Updesh	Binni/Pillo Balwinder	Doddo Khushdev	Shindi Amarjit
					Bhappi Jaihind		Kuku Gurbinder
					Pali Inderpal		
					Kamal Kawal Neni		
					Kinney Navkiran		

Children's nicknames (top line), their given names (bottom line)

Introduction

Part one of the book describes the early years of our father, Kartar Singh Sumal's life in colonial East Africa after landing there in 1927. It provides an insight to an Indian migrant's joys, adventures and struggles to start a new life in the heart of Africa among the local people and the new migrants from Europe. It is based on the personal details left behind by our father, via audio tapes in Punjabi and written records in English. After compiling information from different sources and translating documents from Punjabi to English, it was decided to write this part in the third person, in order to allow the reader a glimpse into the thoughts and motivations of Kartar.

Part two of the book contains translations of letters written to Kartar in East Africa by his two brothers Gurmukh and Shangara in India, during a six-year period from 1943 to 1949. The letters take us back on a personal journey, reliving the dynamics of a joint farming family in a small village in Punjab. After arriving in East Africa in 1925, Gurmukh left the country twice to resettle in India and Shangara did the same once. The two brothers' return to East Africa in 1943 was hindered by changes in East Africa's immigration rules. They finally returned to settle in East Africa for good in 1947 and 1949, respectively. The letters bring to life the family's struggles, and how their overwhelming unity, love and support for each other ultimately helped them to survive the challenges. They provide a personal angle on history and give us a glimpse into the private lives and intimate thoughts of the writers. These plain-spoken letters with beautiful descriptive details, draw the reader into the physical and emotional experience of the day-to-day life of farming families in small villages of Punjab in the 1940s. They show how the hearts of three brothers remained connected and intertwined, despite the thousands of miles separating them. They recapture an era when written correspondence was supreme.

The family's migration to East Africa was for economic reasons. The early death of their father resulted in a rapid deterioration of the family's financially privileged life. As seen in the letters, it is interesting to note, how the three brothers took over three distinct roles of their father after his death. Gurmukh stepped into the shoes of his father as a well-respected head of the family, always taking pride in the success and unity of the whole family. Kartar became the steady breadwinner through his hard work and ability to make practical and astute decisions about his future, just like his mother. Shangara took over the responsibility for practical and technical tasks, always willing to help others. In Kenya, his sharp brain, combined with sincere hard work, helped him to climb the promotion ladder in his post-office job. Shangara was the only family member whose senior ranking earned him entitlement to first class sea travel when he returned to India in 1964 after his retirement. The fourth brother Gurdial always remained the well-loved baby of the family.

This book is a prequel to "Leave Only Footprints" written by one of the authors, Jaihind S Sumal. Some of the information overlaps with Kartar's memoirs in the earlier book

Indian Migrants in East Africa

During the main migration period from India to East Africa (1910-1950), most families in India lived in a joint family system, where parents, sons with their wives and children and unmarried daughters all lived under one roof. The eldest son, as head of the family, would control the finances, decision making and other paternal responsibilities. Younger sons and their wives had little say in family matters. This often led to both perceived and actual unfairness of distribution of food and other privileges between families within this joint system. The friction caused by the unfairness far exceeded the advantages of communal living.

The initial Indian immigrants to East Africa were mostly male, single and under the age of thirty. After a short stay they would return to India for an arranged marriage to a girl selected by the family back home. Brides arriving in East Africa had been brought up in joint families and were accustomed to systems where they and sometimes even their parents, had little say in family decisions. In East Africa, they took over full responsibilities of bringing up a family. This gave them the opportunity to provide for and bring up their families the way they wanted. They were responsible for daily household expenses like food and clothes for the family, and for the schooling and disciplining of their children. Large families were the norm in those days so hiring African domestic helps gave them the much-needed break from menial domestic tasks, allowing them the time to concentrate on their families. It was a young Indian society, with hardly any grandparents around and very few close relatives, sparing the young mothers from judgmental and critical opinions on ways to raise their children. They shared their experiences and relied on each other to learn the various skills needed to run a household and raise a family in their adopted country. Their reliance on mutual support and guidance led to strong bonds between the young families, thus creating a very close-knit Indian community in East Africa.

Although these young mothers felt homesick and missed their families back home, they had a very difficult time adjusting to a joint family life, when they visited India, especially for a longer period. They felt eager to return to their independent lives in East Africa. This message comes out strongly through these letters.

The second-generation Indian children in East Africa grew up in a very protective environment. It was a healthy upbringing with good nourishment and schooling. The absence of crime allowed them to spend more time in independent outdoor activities with their peers. Children watched out for each other. The younger ones learned from the older ones, who provided guidance and protection. This minimal need for parental supervision helped them to become confident, independent and responsible.

After the early struggles of settling in East Africa, a comfortable life was established. The parents with more free time were able to help and motivate their children to excel in education, each new age group doing better than the previous one. This created an environment of healthy competition and the added encouragement from parents gave the children a good foundation to progress further. The Indians born in East Africa stepped easily into well paid professional careers when they migrated to Western countries after East Africa's independence. The protective and comfortable environment in which East African Indians excelled in education led them to do well in their selected professions in their adopted countries, but they failed to become inspired to reach leadership positions. They lacked the fiercely ambitious aspirations of their Indian counterparts from the sub-continent, whose motivation to quickly rise to leadership roles was a direct result of the economic challenges and fierce competition they had faced in order to attain their education.

From 1910 to 1950, the economic status and education levels of Indians continued to improve in East Africa. It was a period of settling down in a new country and adapting to British institutions. The new generation was exposed to the influences of Western education and better economic standards. These factors brought about greater East Africanization of Indian immigrants and the gradual decline of their initial strong links with India. A distinct East African Indian culture emerged that was neither African, Western nor Indian but a mix of all three. This diaspora was particularly distinct for the younger generation born and brought up in East Africa. The new generation's desire to speak with a British accent and to distance themselves from the English spoken with an Indian accent while not losing touch with their Indian mother tongues and culture, made them stand out from their equally well-educated counterparts in India.

Similarly, the first generation of older immigrants started to feel like permanent settlers with the passage of time, getting accustomed to the comfortable lifestyle in East Africa. Good prospects of employment and economic improvement attracted more settlers with an increasing stake in the territories. Indians in East Africa came from rural areas with a wide range of backgrounds and brought their own little rituals and traditions with them. In the melting pot in East Africa, most of these rituals and traditions were amalgamated and lost, except for wedding ceremonies which varied according to different religions. The Indian generation born in East Africa had little knowledge of the Indian caste system.

PART 1
Pioneering Days of an Indian Railway Worker in East Africa (1928 - 1942)

Kartar certainly lived up to the meaning of his Punjabi name, "master of creation" or "creative like God", as is evident from his life captured in this book. His fantastic sense of humor always got the better of him even in his old age. Whenever his grandchildren asked the meaning of his name, he would always reply with a twinkle in his eyes "Send telegram", the literal meaning of the words Kar [Send] tar [telegram]! He was born on April 15, 1912 into the well-to-do family of a civil servant. The family fortunes took a turn for the worse after their father's death. Looking for ways to support her family, the widowed mother had to make the difficult decision to send her young sons to newly opened African countries to earn a living and provide for the family left behind. Kartar's seventeen-year-old brother Gurmukh and nineteen-year-old sister Karam left for East Africa in early 1925, to join Karam's husband Hukam who was settled in Kenya. Kartar followed them almost three years later, and left Bombay on December 16, 1927 on the S.S. Alora, at the age of fifteen.

CHAPTER 1

1927
Arrival in East Africa

First Glimpse of Africa

"**B**ato shay" [Those are lights] said someone in Gujarati, near the front starboard railings of S.S. Alora. "Nathi taro shay" [No, those are stars] replied another, from a small group of Indians gathered on the deck. They were all in their late teens and twenties. Their eager eyes were fixed on the western horizon, dimly lit by a waxing crescent moon. Kartar was fast asleep, lying on a dhari [homespun cotton mat] on the deck, feeling cozy under a khes [cotton blanket] in the cool breeze of the night, after a warm humid evening. On December 26, 1927, a ten-day-long journey had brought them from the Indian port of Bombay [Mumbai] to the vicinity of the African port of Mombasa. It was just after midnight and the crowd had gathered for their first glimpse of their future country, future way of life and, most importantly, their future home. As the passengers gathered, the commotion on the deck and the excited talk about the approaching land got louder.

Kartar woke up and gazed sleepily towards the rails. He could see dim lights in the distance, far fewer than those they had left behind at the port of Bombay. He quickly rolled up his bedding and tied a string tightly around it. He was traveling with a group of youngsters from his village and its surrounding areas. They had all pooled together and had collectively bought rations for the journey. The leftover charcoal for cooking was tossed over the ship's rails and food rations in the kitchen had already been divided amongst the group. Kartar's portion was now packed in his suitcase with his other belongings. A quick wash and a change of clothes from kurta pajama into a

new cotton trouser suit, a parting gift from his mother, soon had him looking smart and confident, ready to take on the challenges of the new country.
Looking around, he noticed that some people were still fast asleep, while
the younger, eager ones had gathered on the deck, looking clean and fresh
in their Sunday best. A buzz of excitement, anticipation and nervousness
was in the air.

Accompanied by the two friends from his village, a Hindu, Chajju Ram
and a Muslim, Rehmat Khan, he walked over to the cooking area where
Rur Singh was pouring tea into brass cups. Rur Singh was their guide and
mentor, as he had done this journey before. They enjoyed their last ship meal
of panjiri [a Punjabi sweet made of flour, ghee and sugar], washed down by
hot tea, before washing and packing away their brass cups and bowls, which
had their names engraved with dotted punch marks for identification. It
was a common Punjabi tradition for maternal grandparents to gift engraved
brass utensils to their newborn grandchild. The child would use and carry
the utensils to adulthood. The excited trio was all packed and ready to take
their first step on an unknown land.

With daybreak, the rays of the sun illuminated the east coast of their
new home, like spotlights on a stage. As the ship slowly advanced towards
the shore, a large shed with a small jetty came into view. On the starboard
side of the ship a sunken ship sticking out of water was visible. A tugboat
followed by some small boats approached the ship. Several uniformed men
boarded the ship. As instructed by the ship's staff, people on the deck started
forming queues, each person tightly clutching a bunch of official looking
papers and a blue British passport. This small blue book defined Kartar as
a 'British Subject' a title which seemed incompatible with his outlook and
patriotic passion for India during his early life. Little did he know that he
would be grateful for this title in his later years, when it opened opportunities around the world for him and his family.

European families from cabins on the upper decks, started coming down
to board the boats, which would take them to the jetty. Some looked the
worse for wear, having indulged in the onboard Christmas party the evening before. With the Europeans safely on their way to the shore, "health
inspection" and immigration checks started for Indians standing patiently

in queues on the deck. Passports and papers for inoculations were checked, followed by a temperature check and a quick glance at their tonsils. Those who passed the tests heaved a sigh of relief and joined the queue for boarding the boats. After a short boat ride to the jetty, Kartar walked purposefully to the shed, each step leaving an imprint in the African soil on which he was destined to spend the next 36 years of his life. On entering the customs shed, all passengers collected their luggage which had been brought in by porters from the ship. The customs inspection was quick as they hardly ever found anything of value in the meager belongings of most Indians, a reflection of the frugal lives they had left behind.

As he stepped out through the doors, it hit Kartar that he was finally in Kenya, a country that he had dreamed of for so long after hearing enticing stories from people visiting his homeland. He wondered if this land of opportunities would be full of surprises and contradictions, a mix of joy and sadness reflecting his journey so far.

First Month in East Africa

With the formalities out of the way, Rur led them on a mile long walk to Tek Singh's house, in Kilindini railway quarters. Rur and Tek Singh had worked together in the railway stores. The excitement and anticipation of the group grew with each stride as the hyped recollections of the morning's events grew louder. Some talked loudly about what was to come, while others, fearing the unknown, listened in silence.

The new arrivals spent the afternoon playing card games under the shade of a mango tree outside Tek Singh's house, before catching the evening train to Nairobi. They were interrupted by a man watching the game, who came over to ask them to break a 20-shilling note for him. The three friends had exchanged 150 rupees each (Rs 450) into shillings. Chajju Ram, the eldest and most responsible, being a family man with a wife and two children back home, kept their passports and collective money in a bag, from which he gave the change to the stranger. Engrossed in the game, they lost track of time until a reminder came from the house. The game ended abruptly when they rushed in to get ready for the train, but soon realized that the bag had been left behind. Chajju ran out to retrieve it, but to his dismay, there was no sign of the bag. They were left penniless and without passports on their first day on African soil!

On the directions of Tek Singh, they sprinted to the police station to report the loss. Faizalali, the police inspector, had previously worked in Kisumu and knew Kartar's brother Gurmukh and his brother-in-law Hukam Singh.

"It will be difficult to recover the money, but we might be able to retrieve the passports, as the perpetrators will probably discard them," said Faizalali.

It was nearly time to catch the train, so the trio hurriedly signed the papers reporting their missing passports but not the money. They had to borrow money from their host Tek Singh for the remaining journey.

Kartar found it difficult to switch off his overactive mind on the train journey to Nairobi and was up at the crack of dawn. He sat by the window, mesmerized by the natural beauty of the African savanna, with its lush green meadows interspersed by acacia trees. Its virgin soil was untouched by the blade of a plow or a hoe, in sharp contrast to Punjab where almost every inch of land was covered with crops, every stem and leaf of which had been cultivated by human hands, leaving no natural open areas for animals to graze. Watching the animals roaming freely in their own kingdom, Kartar's young mind, full of dreams for a new future in an unknown country, turned to wondering if he too would have a similar freedom to choose his future.

Little did he know that over the next 34 years he would take this journey back and forth hundreds, if not thousands of times, by the end of which, the familiarity with this stretch of the line would enable him to guess the mile marker, just from the view outside.

After spending a night at a Nairobi Hindu temple, the trio traveled through the Rift Valley to the shores of Lake Victoria for a much-awaited reunion with Kartar's elder sister, Karam Kaur, in Kisumu. The next morning, they set sail on a small ship SS Clement Hill, to arrive at Jinja at the end of the day, after a short stopover at Majanji. A short train ride from Jinja took them to their destination Namasagali on the shores of the river Nile, near Lake Kyoga (also spelled as Kioga), in Uganda. Kartar's brother Gurmukh was waiting for him at the station. Meeting his brother after three years, filled the 15-year-old teenager with an excitement which was difficult for him to contain. They gave each other a long tight hug.

THE PURPLE LINE ON THE MAP SHOWS THE ROUTE FOR
KARTAR'S JOURNEY FROM MOMBASA TO NAMASAGALI

The two brothers shared a cold room made of wood with a corrugated tin roof as opposed to the warm mud-walled rooms lapped with cow dung, in India. Lying on a cotton dhari [cotton mat], they wrapped themselves in a razai [quilt from India] to stay warm during cold nights. It felt odd to lie on a bed surface made of hessian sack after the jute or cotton string woven surfaces of Indian beds. Somehow, carrying a blanket or razai with them made most Indians feel better prepared for venturing into colder foreign countries. This tradition carried on into the 1960's when Indians were commonly seen carrying folded blankets on their arms while flying to the UK.

Other oddities that struck Kartar were that rainwater was collected in big tanks for daily domestic use, instead of the Indian way of drawing water from wells, and kerosine lamps were used as opposed to mainly candles in India. Europeans, leaving behind their comforts and amenities such as running water, sewerage and electricity, saw the rough living in Africa as an adventure. For the Indians, moving to Africa was an upgrade in life's comforts, with easily accessible water in tanks, instead of having to fetch it from a well, and daily sewage collection from buckets in toilets eliminating the need to go outside to relieve themselves.

For Kartar, the first month in a new place, new country, new continent, felt more like a dream and it passed by quickly, despite its ups and downs.

CHAPTER 2

1928
Life in Jinja

Determination to Pull Out of Dark Days

After celebrating a quiet new year with his brother, it didn't take long for the reality of his new situation to sink in. Kartar missed his family and the happy familiar surroundings of his village in India. He felt bewildered amid three different cultures in this strange country, two of which, the British and East African cultures, were completely alien to him. He felt very lonely after his brother and his young Indian mates left for work early in the mornings. Even the two friends who had accompanied Kartar from the village, had found work with the railways as handymen. Kartar, with his high school education, deserved a job with better prospects. Returning home was too expensive. Life was closing in on him from all sides. Depression set in, which is reflected in the very first letter from Kartar's brother in-law in Nairobi to his brother in Namasagali

From Hukam Singh in Nairobi to Gurmukh Singh
in Namasagali, dated 25.2.1928

Bhai Saab Gurmukh Singh Ji, Sat Siri Akal

I received your telegram in which you wrote that Kartar Singh is not keeping well and is not interested in learning. Please do not send him to Nairobi unless he has learnt telegraphy. Without these skills he will have no chance of employment in Nairobi. The idea of him joining the Railway Telegraphy School will not work as they do not admit students with no basic knowledge. Again, it is very important that he learns telegraphy before coming here and then I will try and see what I can do regarding his employment. If he does not want to learn telegraphy, then he can learn some kind of trade and work as a 'fundi' [handyman] like his friend Chajju. If he comes here without learning a trade, then I cannot do anything to help him.

With reference to him constantly being ill, there might be a doctor near you who can treat him for free but, here in Nairobi we will have to pay for his treatment. Living expenses here are high, his food will cost at least 40 shillings a month, plus other overhead expenses of 10-20 shillings. It will be difficult for me to afford to keep him here with us. So, you decide what should be done, I am giving you my opinion. I just wanted to make you aware that we will be incurring unnecessary expenses, without any benefit to anyone. I hope you won't feel offended by this.

Another matter I feel compelled to mention is that we need to pay our kisht [installment] by 6 March, so I will be grateful if you can send us money, whatever you can spare. We will really appreciate it if you can send Sh 500, of which Sh 200 will be returned to you as soon as we are able to. We need this money urgently.

Please return the Doctor's lottery book with unsold tickets. The draw for the winning prize of a bicycle will take place soon.

You have written that Kartar Singh and his companions' stolen passports have been received but something needs to be done about the money that got stolen. They only reported the theft of three passports to Mombasa Police and did not mention the missing money. If we ask the Police at this stage, they will want to know why the stolen money was not included in the original report so nothing can be done now.

Narain Singh, who was a station master at Ruiru, had Blackwater fever. His brother brought him to Nairobi for treatment, but sadly he did not survive. The news of his death is very sad but us mortals can't do anything about such things. It is all in Parmatma's [God's] hands. Narain Singh recently got married in India and his wife is still there. I don't know what will become of his widow now.

Everyone over here is fine.

Reply soon.
Dass, Hukam Singh

This letter was written three months after Kartar's arrival in Uganda and mentions his health and lack of interest. It was most probably homesickness as he was just a kid in a country three and a half thousand miles away from his home and family.

At the time, their brother-in-law Hukam Singh worked for a bank in Nairobi. His wife Karam Kaur, who was their elder sister, was living on a family farm in Kisumu. The letter asks Gurmukh Singh to send 300 shillings. Was this money to pay back a loan for Kartar's fare for the journey from India? Kartar's monthly pay when he started work was 150 shillings, so 300 shillings would be nearly two months' wages.

At that time Africans and Asians were not allowed to own commercial farms and could only grow food for personal consumption. Asian farms in the Kisumu area were an exception to this rule. Europeans could farm on a commercial basis and they mainly grew crops for export to the UK. This must have contributed to high food prices in Nairobi, apparently almost a third of an Indian's salary.

The mortgage payment was most likely for the farm Hukam and his two brothers had bought in Kisumu.

HUKAM SINGH ON THEIR FAMILY FARM IN KISUMU, 1960s

The letter refers to lottery tickets with a bicycle as the winning prize, which must have been a very attractive prize in those days in order to warrant the sale of tickets in several towns in Kenya.

The cost of a bicycle was the same as two months' salary, so very few Indians could afford it. Kartar learnt to ride a bike in 1929, when his friend Ramlal left his bicycle and other belongings with Kartar for safekeeping, before departing for India on a three-month long leave.

First Paid Job and Sickness

The family had sacrificed their meager income to pay for Kartar's fare for the journey. He could not let them down, so he overcame his fears, pulled himself together and started learning telegraphy from his brother, who worked as a telegraphist for the railways. Gurmukh spoke to the Namasagali station master Desai about Kartar's employment, who in turn introduced him to the Railway District Superintendent Lawson. Gurmukh helped Kartar to write a job application letter, as he had a better command of the English language, having been in the country for three years. The letter, which mentioned Kartar's knowledge of telegraphy and three years of high school education, was sent off to Lawson, along with his High School character and academic reports. Within a fortnight Kartar received a job offer, asking him to report to the station master in Jinja. At the time the Jinja to Kampala rail line was being built and the material for the line was being transported to Jinja by ship from the Port of Kisumu. This opened job opportunities at Jinja.

Kartar started his first job in Jinja as a train clerk. A train clerk's duties included keeping account of goods loaded and unloaded from ships and trains and communicating this information via telegraph to the receiving and dispatching train stations. The job suited Kartar's good mathematical skills, and it required limited spoken English, in which Kartar was not yet fluent. He started work on May 17, 1928, at the age of sixteen, for 150 Kenyan shillings per month. In his desperation to earn a living Kartar put a false date of birth on his application to meet the minimum requirement of eighteen for employment.

In Jinja, Kartar moved into a single room shared with three other bachelors, one of whom was Inder Singh Gill. All of them sent most of their wages to families in India, and would run out of rations towards the end of the month, when they lived on potatoes only. Inder Singh Gill came up with the plan of tying a string to their individual potatoes while boiling them, to establish a "potato identity." He also taught them to split matchsticks lengthwise to make a matchbox last twice as long. Kartar continued to scrimp and save in order to send money regularly to the family left behind in India.

The joy of a new job and a new beginning did not last long. A month into the job, Kartar had his first attack of potentially fatal Blackwater fever, an acute form of malaria, which causes high temperature followed by the passing of blackish urine. He followed the only treatment available, to drink lots of liquids, mainly water and an occasional lassi [yogurt-based cooling drink] or carbonated soda, to flush out the system. His neighbor Ramlal Bowrey's wife and her brother took care of him. His brother Gurmukh's visit greatly boosted his morale. Dr Shadiram Mohindru and his assistant Ahamadeen Ahmadi treated him. To prevent his kidneys from rupturing, he was advised to rest lying on his back, which gave him a bed sore. It took Kartar two months to get back on his feet. Migrants lacked immunity and were very susceptible to tropical diseases.

Visit from a Future King

On returning to work after recovering from his illness, Kartar sensed a buzz of excitement in the air. Preparations were in full swing for the impending visit of Prince of Wales [later King Edward VIII, who abdicated the British throne to marry American socialite Wallis Simpson]. Banners and flags were arranged and rearranged. The welcoming band practiced over and over, until they were perfect. After visiting Makerere University in Uganda on August 10, 1928, a forty-mile drive on a dark red dirt road took the Prince from Kampala to Bugungu, with its ferry ramp on Lake Victoria, also called Victoria Nyanza. A mile of water separated them from their destination, the Jinja Ferry ramp. The short journey on a ferry brought them to Jinja Pier [present day home of Jinja sailing club]. At the time, for a road journey, the ferry was the only crossing point connecting the two halves of Uganda which were split by the river Nile.

A few local Indian dukawalas [shopkeepers], mostly Gujaratis and two other Sikhs with turbans, besides Kartar, were selected to greet the prince. Perhaps, the turbans were seen as a more visual representation of Indians as defending warriors of the Empire. They were fully trained on how to address the prince, if spoken to.

Early in the morning, on the big day, Kartar walked to the Jinja Ferry ramp, less than a mile away from Jinja train station. In the warmth of the sun, he felt fresh, smart and confident, wearing a turban and his one and only cotton suit over a white shirt. He had washed them days earlier and had ironed his suit and shirt the evening before. Everyone started taking their designated places on a small, paved area attached to the ramp. In the line-up, Kartar stood between Hari Singh, who worked for the Public Works Department and Kala Singh, an inspector for rail lines. After a long wait in the hot sun, they saw a ferry coming towards them. It was a flat-bottomed barge, with a smaller steam barge tied alongside. The well decorated barges carried two cars. After a few traditional ceremonies, presentations and introductions, the prince started walking past the line-up. He stopped in front of Kartar, whose youthful smart appearance as a sixteen-year-old, probably made him stand out.

Kartar bowed to the prince.

"Punjabi hai? [Are you Punjabi?]" asked the prince.

"Yes, your Royal Highness" answered Kartar.

"Bohut accha hai [That is good]" he replied.

Kartar felt very proud of that encounter with the future king of Britain.

From Jinja, the Prince continued on a 140 miles journey to Masindi, a small town between Lake Kyoga and Lake Albert, and gateway to the famous Murchison Falls and the parks around it. Masindi with its newly built Masindi Hotel, a rustic single-story building, was the most suitable lodging for the prince to spend the night.

Later that evening the prince decided to go and visit a local village on his own without informing his entourage. He wanted to see and experience the lives of the local people. When he failed to return by nightfall, everyone feared for his safety, and telegraphs were sent to several locations. That is when Kartar got to read a telegram sent to the authorities in Jinja. The search continued through the night. According to rumors, the prince had his dinner with a local African family and had rested in one of their huts. His arrival at the hotel early in the morning was a big relief for security personnel. Telexes were sent out confirming his safe return.

KARTAR IN HIS COTTON SUIT, A PARTING GIFT FROM HIS MOTHER. FOR A MAN
WHO WAS ALWAYS IMPECCABLY DRESSED, THE THREE DIFFERENT BUTTONS
APPEAR INCONGRUOUS. THIS WAS MOST LIKELY DUE TO THE SCARCITY OF
TAILORS OR SEWING ACCESSORIES DURING THAT ERA OF MAINLY BACHELOR
INDIANS RESIDING IN EAST AFRICA. THIS IS AMPLY ILLUSTRATED IN THE 1940S
LETTERS FROM HIS BROTHERS, WHICH MENTION THE NECESSITY FOR GETTING
THEIR CLOTHES STITCHED IN INDIA BEFORE DEPARTING FOR EAST AFRICA

Loneliness and Homesickness

After his father's death, Kartar's Naniji [maternal grandmother] had moved in with the family. She doted on Kartar and her deep love was reciprocated by young Kartar. She was very sad when Kartar departed for Africa and gave him a lock of her hair, as a keepsake. As promised, Kartar kept this treasure in a small container, and would carefully open it to connect with his Naniji, whenever he missed her. One night while sleeping next to his brother, Kartar dreamt of his Naniji being cremated, and started muttering while tossing and turning in distress. His brother shook him awake, lit the kerosene lamp, brought him a glass of water and admonished him to calm down while reminding him that it was only a dream. Three days later they received a telegram that their Naniji had died. For a long time, this incident caused a conflict in Kartar's mind as he was a non-believer in the supernatural.

For Kartar, who was grieving for his dear grandmother, illness and loneliness finally took their toll. Worries of his family's financial difficulties on top of his own struggles in this strange, difficult and sometimes hostile environment, felt difficult to handle. Then came another blow to his morale, when the two travel companions from his village got homesick after a few months and returned to India. Disease, homesickness and attacks by wild animals drove a lot of young migrants back to India.

Kartar could not keep his mind off his predicament. Returning to India was not an option for him as he could not let his mother down. He felt very vulnerable, thousands of miles away from home, surrounded by disease and people whose languages and traditions he could not grasp. He needed some quiet time to himself. To get away from the hustle and bustle of the train station, he went and sat down in a coach on the train. Memories of his family and the carefree life he had left behind in India, less than a year ago overwhelmed Kartar and brought tears to his eyes. His boss Lawson, who was walking along the platform, saw his new young employee crying. He climbed onto the train and sat opposite Kartar. They started talking and Kartar explained in his broken English that he felt lonely and missed his family back home and his brother in Namasagali. Lawson knew Gurmukh from when he had worked in Namasagali [54 miles away from Jinja]. He promised Kartar that if a job opening came up, he would transfer him to be with his elder brother.

On the fourth of December Kartar was transferred to Namasagali as assistant Pier Clerk. The completion of the Tororo to Mbulamuti line in January 1929 provided a direct rail link from Mombasa to Jinja and Namasagali. Kartar, and other staff members were transferred to different locations, in anticipation of reduced goods being loaded at Jinja.

Kartar was very happy to be reunited with his brother. The joyful reunion felt great and helped Kartar to feel more positive about his situation. It did not take him long to settle down in a more stable and predictable lifestyle.

It had been a difficult year for Kartar in a new country, with an entirely alien culture and lifestyle, thousands of miles away from home!

CHAPTER 3

1929
Settling Down in Namasagali

Kartar's brother, Gurmukh was transferred to Lugazi in early 1929. By that time Kartar was well integrated into a close-knit group of Gurmukh's friends. After his brother's departure, a mutual friend Prahlad Singh, who later owned Sikh Sawmills in Tanzania, moved in as his roommate.

First European Friend

Edward, an Englishman, had a contract to supply food [mainly fish and meat from small animals] to the Railways catering service serving the trains and ships that docked in Namasagali. Ships on the East African lakes connected terminal points on railways and came under the Railways' jurisdiction. As assistant pier clerk, Kartar was also responsible for supplies received from Edward. With their almost daily business interactions, Edward and Kartar soon became good friends.

Edward lived with his wife in a small house near the point where the river Nile enters Lake Kyoga. Fish in large numbers, moving with the flow of the river, entered the open waters of the lake, which were rich in nutrients. Their concentration was high at this neck point where Edward lived. Edward did spear-fishing at night using long thin sticks sharpened at one end. The catch was mainly to sell to the Railways. He used a kerosene lamp to light up his small motorboat. Once the boat was in the open water, he would place the lamp at the open end of a long pipe, in order to illuminate the other end, which was under water. The illuminated water below the boat, exposed the fish, thus enabling Edward to pierce them with his sharpened sticks before hauling them onto his boat. In an hour's trip on the water, he could easily catch 20 to 30 large fish.

Occasionally on Saturday evenings, Kartar and his Irish boss Sean (Head Pier Clerk) accompanied Edward on his fishing trips. At the time, in early 1929, Kartar had been away from home for just over a year and it was his first opportunity to be with English speaking companions and converse with them. In his Indian high school education, he had learnt to read and write in English but lacked oral skills. His two previous jobs of keeping a record of goods, required only occasional spoken English. At the age of seventeen, these outings provided a great opportunity to learn British ways and improve his English communication skills.

One clear moonlit Saturday night, the three of them, Edward, Sean and Kartar, set out on a fishing expedition. Edward had a large order to deliver so they were out on the lake for a long time. As their boat approached the shore at around three in the morning, they saw a hippo near the water's edge. Seeing that the hippo was alone, Edward got excited and wanted to hunt it for its meat. He moved the boat towards the shore, a few hundred feet from the water's edge, where the hippo stood. Edward jumped out into waist deep water, holding a shotgun above his head and waded his way to the shore. Unseen by any of them, there was another hippo lurking behind a bush at the point where Edward came ashore. This second hippo rushed to topple Edward over and started mauling him between its front legs and chest. After a few minutes, both hippos walked away leaving the badly injured Edward lying on the shore. Neither Sean nor Kartar had any experience of starting or controlling a motorboat. Kartar pulled the rope on the boat engine, the way he had seen Edward, and the engine roared to life. They slowly navigated the boat nearer to the shore, and stepped out gingerly, shivering from the cold water and the fear of what awaited them on the hippo and crocodile infested shore. In the light of a full moon, they could see Edward's blood covered face and were relieved to see him move his leg, a sign that he was alive.

Keeping a lookout for any movements in the bushes, they carried Edward onto the boat, and somehow managed to navigate it towards Namasagali pier, where they pulled it ashore near the Pier Master, Archibald's house.

Mr Archibald accompanied Kartar to the pier's 'First Aid' station to pick up a stretcher and to call the local doctor, Dr Noor Mohammad. On seeing the patient, the doctor advised them to take him to Jinja, fifty miles away, to a 'whites only' hospital. Edward, lying on a stretcher in the back of a van, was rushed to the hospital. This is when Kartar, who accompanied him, learnt that Edward's wife was away in England to see her family. A medical examination revealed that Edward had broken his ribs and arm and had lacerations on his head and legs. After two to three hours the English doctor attending him came out and told Kartar that Edward's condition was serious but stable. He was then moved to a general ward where Kartar was allowed to visit him.

Looking at Edward lying on the hospital bed, with bandages on his head and legs and a cast on his chest and arm, Kartar could relate to the emptiness and the pain of loneliness in Edward's life, so he requested the head nurse to allow him to stay and look after Edward until his wife's return. Kartar stayed in Jinja for ten days with his brother's friend Karam Singh and spent the nights looking after Edward in hospital. On his return to Namasagali, he received a letter from the District Commissioner in Jinja, thanking him for his help in Edward's case. That letter from the DC, a high post in the British governing system in the colonies, helped Kartar a few times to gain favors in transfers and job selections.

Edward returned home to Namasagali a month later. Kartar became good friends with the couple and they would occasionally invite him for a meal. On 6th June, Edward sold his shotgun to Kartar for 50 shillings, so Kartar started hunting on Sundays, for fowls and other wild birds and small animals. In India they never had meat at home because they couldn't afford it, but the meat from the hunt and an occasional fish from Edward became the main source of Kartar's nourishment. A big change in lifestyle in just over a year.

Meeting an Indian Freedom Fighter

Namasagali was the gateway to Lake Kyoga, Murchison Falls and Lake Albert, a haven for tourists. For the more adventurous visitors it was the start of a journey to Egypt along the river Nile. For an occasional Belgian government official or businessman, it was an easier way to get to the Eastern Belgian Congo, Rwanda and Burundi.

Tuesdays always brought a buzz of excitement to the sleepy town of Namasagali. The train station and the harbor were spruced up and cleared of debris, in preparation for the steamer to dock and the train to arrive from Nairobi. The Tuesday train arriving from Nairobi had two first class corridor coaches which had been attached at Mbulamuti, to the back of a third-class train from Jinja. The two steamers, Stanley or Grant would arrive on alternate Tuesdays. It was Kartar's duty to ensure that the luggage from the first-class train and the steamer passengers reached the correct destinations. The locals, both Europeans and Indians, got all decked up in their best clothes, trying to match the stylish attire and refined mannerism of the new arrivals. The luxurious lifestyle of Europeans was something Indians could only dream of, being fully aware that it would just remain a fantasy and nothing more, due to their limited means. Still, they took pleasure in noticing the full details of how the travelers dressed and behaved. The explorers, appropriately dressed in their safari outfits for adventures in deep Africa, were easy to distinguish from the more elegantly dressed Europeans who were there to enjoy luxury tours and the scenic beauty of the lakes and surrounding area. Officials and businessmen, mostly Belgian, looked smart and ready for business in their suits and ties.

The Indians in the third-class coaches of the train were usually residents returning from a trip or arrivals wanting to start a new life in the area. News of a pending new arrival traveled fast within the community. One day a well-dressed Indian Sikh in his forties got off the first-class coach of the train. His refined mannerism, smart western clothes and neatly tied white turban made him stand out from the crowd. Kartar usually knew all Indians arriving at the station, but this man was a complete surprise. Kartar approached him to take care of his luggage.

A "Sat Siri Akal" [Sikh greeting] was followed by small talk. This well-educated man was from Amritsar in India and his name was Lal Singh. He asked about the Sikh community in town.

"There are six of us in Namasagali. We would feel honored if you could join us for a meal" replied Kartar.

"Yes, I would like to meet the rest of your friends. I must be back here before the ship sails tonight, at eleven" he replied.

"Why don't you spend the rest of the day with us, and we will make sure you are back here on time" Kartar suggested.

After a short rest, a wash and a change of clothes at Kartar's humble abode, which he shared with Prahlad Singh, Lal Singh sat down for tea with the six Sikh friends, who were all dying to know who he was and the purpose of his journey. Swaran asked the pertinent question.

Lal Singh hesitated for a moment before replying

"I feel I can trust you as my fellow countrymen and wish to encourage you to support our cause."

He continued "I am forty-five years old, a freedom fighter. I left India using a false passport and traveled under the pretext of being a rich business-man. I am planning to travel up the Nile to Egypt and from there to Greece and Russia. The Russians will help us in our cause. British controlled check-points everywhere, have made it very difficult for Indian freedom fighters to reach Russia via the normal land route through Afghanistan or via sea. Hence, the reason for taking this unusual route, to avoid getting caught."

"How do you know the Russians will help us?" asked Prahlad

"No one else is prepared to help. Only Russia will stand up to British Imperialism" answered Lal Singh, citing a verse, which he said originated from the times of the Sikh Gurus. It started with the words:

"When the Russians arrive in Punjab

There will be no shortage of grain

And my Sikhs will not suffer any more."

In the conversation that followed, Kartar and his friends felt concerned to learn that he was a member of the Communist Party in India and could speak the Russian language fluently. They diverted the topic of discussion and accompanied him to the ship. In the evening, there used to be dinner and dance parties on the ship for passengers and local Europeans, before its departure. Watching Europeans boarding the ship in their elegant evening gowns and suits, disappearing into a totally unknown world, had always made Kartar wonder what that alien world of glitz and glamor was like, the ticket to which was skin color.

By the time they arrived, the festivities aboard the ship were dying down and the ship was getting ready to sail. A few days later the "Pier Master" Mr. Archibald summoned Kartar and his friends to his office. The authorities had informed him about Lal Singh's activities so he interrogated them individually about his background, the name he traveled under and his possible connections to the local community.

"The only reason I took him home was because he was a fellow Sikh" an honest statement from Kartar did not shed any light on the strange visitor.

Later, they learnt that at one time, Lal Singh had been the editor of a communist paper in India, called 'Kirti'. The topic never came up in their conversations with the authorities. Thoughts of the five hours spent in the company of a mysterious gentleman with a familiar Indian background, but very different strong communist beliefs, stayed in their hearts for a long time. How far did he go, and what did he achieve, they never knew!

Close Encounter with a Crocodile

The group of six friends had rented a single room in a building for Indian workers, to convert it into a prayer room which served as a religious meeting place. This was not just for spiritual reasons, but more to promote a sense of belonging. Sikh holy days were celebrated on the Sundays following the actual occasions, by reciting Sikh prayers and placing garlands of fresh flowers around Guru Granth Sahib, the holy book. The following Sunday, the wilted garlands were placed in the flowing water of the river Nile, half a mile away. This ritual was usually carried out during daylight hours, due to fear of crocodiles and hippos.

Once Kartar and his friend decided to take the wilted garlands to the river on a weekday evening, instead of waiting until Sunday. They followed a narrow path between thick bushes to reach the muddy shores of the river. In the dusk, Kartar could just about make out the silhouette of his friend Karam walking ahead. Karam stepped out casually onto the shore, and felt something wriggling under his feet, just as a large mud-pile rose, revealing a huge crocodile underneath. The crocodile got up on its feet, turning its head towards them. That is the last thing the terrified duo remembered, as they raced away, screaming. It was a close shave and despite Kartar's attempts to put the encounter behind him, the incident caused him to become the butt of many jokes among the Sikh group of friends.

Rituals in Remote Corners

Kartar was familiar with stern wheel paddle steamers Speke, Stanley and Grant, which sailed to and from Namasagali port. Speke carried goods like cotton etc. on barges attached to the front of the steamers. African passengers traveled on the barges. Besides carrying goods, Stanley and Grant had passenger cabins. Stanley had six first class and four second class cabins on the upper deck.

SWS STANLEY

The only piece missing in Britain's desire for a back door route from Mombasa to Egypt was the shipping connection in Lake Albert, an alternative route to protect the Suez Canal, the main shipping connection to its Empire. For this, Britain had built S.S. Robert Coryndon in England, which was then disassembled in order to be shipped to Butiaba on Lake Albert, where the pieces were reassembled. Towards the end of 1929, some disassembled parts and equipment for assembly started arriving in Kenya, ready to be transported to Butiaba. A need to control the inventory of ship parts arriving in Butiaba resulted in Kartar's transfer to Butiaba.

Kartar never had the opportunity to travel on any of the ships on the lake, until he was assigned this job in Butiaba for a couple of months. The seventeen-year-old Kartar got his belongings together, totally unaware of the magnitude of the project in which he would play a small part. Climbing aboard S.S. Stanley with his belongings, was a totally different experience from his previous boardings as an assistant Pier Clerk. He placed his bags in his second-class cabin and joined the others to watch the steamer sail away at 11pm. The passengers formed a strange mix of the usual tourists mixed with workers for assembling the ship. Kartar and his fellow workers stayed on deck to watch the steamer navigate its way through the mighty Nile. He then walked to the rear of the steamer, to watch the stern wheel paddles rotating, before retiring to his cabin.

By morning the steamer was in the middle of Lake Kyoga, the shores of which were covered in swampy grass, with no sign of life. To Kartar, having his morning breakfast served at a table felt like a once-in-a-lifetime luxury, in sharp contrast to sitting down on a low stool on the floor to consume his usual self-cooked simple Indian breakfast.

Around lunchtime the swampy grass shores drew closer, as the steamer finally left Lake Kyoga to sail down the other side of the river Nile. A few hours of maneuvering through the Nile brought the boat to Masindi Port, which was approximately two hundred yards long, with a docking platform and a few small buildings. A bus was waiting to take the passengers to Masindi. Kartar looked forward to his first bus journey in Africa. The front seats were reserved for Europeans only, so Kartar made himself comfortable on a rear seat. He enjoyed the 30 miles of a bumpy ride on dirt roads. The dirt track on the red soil was visible from the front seats but all Kartar could see at the rear was a huge swirling cloud of red dust chasing the bus. It was evening by the time the bus reached Masindi and parked in front of the Masindi Hotel, the same hotel where Prince Edward had stayed a year earlier, after visiting Jinja. The tourists and European workers went into the hotel. Kartar quietly slipped away to sit on a bench outside, fully aware that the charges of the hotel were way beyond his means.

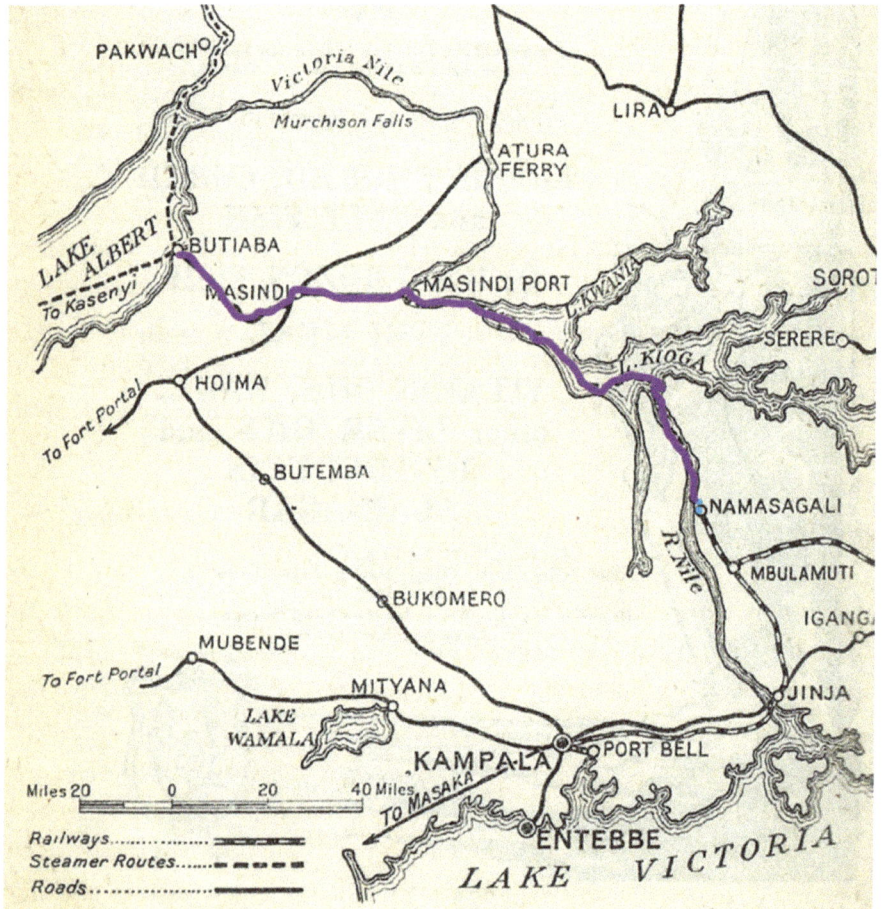

THE PURPLE LINE ON THE MAP SHOWS THE ROUTE FOR
KARTAR'S JOURNEY FROM NAMASAGALI TO BUTIABA

M ASINDI H OTEL

After a short break, the bus left Masindi with Kartar and the European workers. The tourists stayed behind at the hotel. The next stop was their destination Butiaba, where the bus route ended. Butiaba was a small frontier settlement with a pier, a large shed, a few temporary structures and a small residential area. Kartar's assignment as assistant Pier Clerk was to take an inventory of goods arriving there, which were mainly small parts and assembly equipment for the S.S. Robert Coryndon.

A flat bottomed, motorized barge at the pier was used for local trips on the lake. The captain had the mandate to enforce law and order at ports of call. One day he received the alarming news that the Lugbara tribe was preparing a body for some form of ritual, witchcraft or cannibalism, in a nearby village. He assembled a small group of local staff including Kartar and askaris [African police constables] to hike to the village for investigation. They reached the location where a body was being prepared amidst some tribal ceremonies. Upon seeing the captain and his team armed with guns, the locals stopped their activities. The captain instructed his men to dig a big hole in the ground, place the body in it and pour liquid phenol over it, of which they had an ample supply as it was used for disinfecting bathrooms and toilets on the ship. To dissuade the locals from digging the body out, they were informed that the liquid was poisonous, and two askaris were left behind on guard.

S.S.ROBERT CORYNDON

A day that had begun in anticipation of new exciting experiences, ended with turmoil in Kartar's heart. This primitive ritual left a mark on his inquisitive and impressionable young mind. He pondered on questions of birth and death. All humans come into the world the same way, from their mother's womb, but different cultures decide how the physical body departs from the world. Kartar wondered if souls leaving their physical forms also followed cultural rules. His faith in God and deep-rooted Indian beliefs had taught him that the soul gets liberated from the physical form during cremation. As his life weaved through different lands, people and cultures, his experiences taught him to lean more towards atheism than having blind faith in a God whose existence was unknown.

After a depressing first year where darkness had enveloped Kartar, he felt more settled and better integrated into life in East Africa, by the end of the second year.

CHAPTER 4

1930 - 1931
Brothers Reunited in Tororo

At that time, Namasagali was a small frontier town, more like a settlement in surroundings where the raw beauty of nature was left untouched by the so-called development. It was the last stop on the railway line from the coast, right in the middle of the great continent of Africa.

In January 1930, Kartar's transfer to Tororo left him with mixed feelings of sadness and joy. Sadness on leaving a beautiful area which had started to feel like a second home to him and joy at being reunited with his brother. Gurmukh had resigned from his Post Office job at the end of 1929 to join the Kenya Uganda Railways as a guard in Tororo. A guard traveled in the caboose of a train and was responsible for controlling and accounting of goods loaded and off loaded, at train stations on the way.

Kartar's transfer from Namasagali to Tororo brought the two brothers under one roof, both working for the same organization. Both felt somewhat established in this new country, having lived there for five and two years, respectively. The game of musical chairs continued when Gurmukh was transferred to Nakuru a year later and then to Nairobi, in Kenya.

The "Great American Recession" of 1929 slowly spread to Britain and its colonies. By 1931, like other organizations, the Railways in East Africa started laying people off, especially in big cities like Nairobi. There was high unemployment, shortage of goods and a drop in incomes. Being new in the country, Indians were disproportionately impacted by the recession and some of them started returning to India. Gurmukh, seeing the writing on the wall, resigned from his job and after a short stay with Kartar in Tororo, returned to India.

CHAPTER 5

1932
Wedding in India

Second Attack of Blackwater Fever in Tororo

Gradually with time, more permanent structures replaced the small temporary humble wooden abodes of earlier Indian settlements. This was especially true in big cities of East Africa. Kartar moved into a house shared with a dozen other Indian Punjabis working for the Railways. Money was pooled together to employ a full time Sikh cook at 100 shillings a month. Free evenings and days were spent playing field hockey, a sport they had brought with them from their mother country. Sunday mornings were for playing matches with teams from surrounding areas. One Sunday morning, just as the team was leaving for Mbale to play a game against their local team, Kartar felt unwell and decided to stay behind. As the day progressed his temperature shot up and when he went to urinate in the late afternoon, he noticed that the urine was thick and black. He knew it was Blackwater fever, a tropical disease with no medical cure except to flush it out of the system by drinking plenty of water. He continued to drink water from a big container placed next to his bed. His friends took care of him, but on the third day, he stopped urinating and started losing consciousness. A local doctor, Dr. Ramford was called. The semi-conscious Kartar vaguely noticed the doctor shaking his head while whispering to his friend Bachitar, before leaving. Kartar knew the end was near.

Kartar's friends sent a telegram to his brother-in-law, Hukam in Kisumu, mentioning the seriousness of his condition. Hukam and his three brothers had bought farming land in Kibos, and grew sugarcane on it. The family owned a late 1920's Ford car with a soft top. As soon as they received the telegram, Kartar's sister Karam, Hukam and their few months old daughter Surjeet, set off for Eldoret in their car. Just after they had passed Kakamega, a small settlement at the halfway point, it started raining hard and the car broke down. The young family had no choice but to sit and wait in the car, hoping for someone to come by. Luckily, just after midnight a truck returning to Tororo after delivering cotton bales to cotton ginneries in Kisumu, stopped by. As it turned out, the Indian Gujarati driver knew Hukam, so he left his African companion to watch the car while he drove the family to Tororo in his truck.

They found Kartar lying on the floor, in accordance with a Hindu-Punjabi tradition of placing a dying person close to mother earth. Kartar's sister sat down beside him, holding his hand and praying for his life, as tears rolled down her cheeks. She was gripped with fear for Kartar's life because Hukam's younger brother Gian Singh Mangat had recently died of Blackwater fever, in Kibos. Hukam requested the truck driver to take him to Dr. Ramford's surgery, which was next-door to his residence, in a beautiful location on top of a hill overlooking the town. The doctor understood the urgency of the situation, and drove down to Kartar's home, with Hukam by his side.

Dr. Ramford decided to try out a new treatment, which was practiced by the locals and in later years became a regular way to treat the disease. Kartar was placed on a bed of woven jute, and wrapped up in blankets, with two hot water bottles on either side. Angithi [an Indian charcoal stove] at a very low heat was placed under his bed. The doctor gave him an injection and asked his sister to keep him hydrated with barley water. Kartar started hallucinating that he was being hung by his feet from a tree in the heat of the sun and his sister was calling out to him. He tried to open his eyes but couldn't.

After a while, he passed urine, wetting his clothes and the blankets, which meant that his kidneys were functioning and there was a chance of recovery. By the evening Kartar had peed several times, so the hot coal and the blankets were removed. He made a good recovery within a week, when his sister and her family returned to Kisumu. The doctor recommended complete rest for him and he was granted 100 days leave to go to India for rehabilitation.

Journey Back Home

On getting the news of Kartar's impending visit to India, his mother had found a bride for him and had performed the engagement ceremony in his absence, by using his turban to represent him.

A number of Kartar's Indian friends were caught up in layoffs in the Railways and were planning to return to India. Kartar left for India in April 1932 with Arjan Singh Mangat and Naginder Singh Gill. They were looking forward to seeing their families, villages and meeting old childhood friends again. All three were engaged and were going to India to get married. They could hardly contain the excitement of seeing their intended brides for the first time, not having seen their photographs. They knew nothing about the young girls they were destined to spend their lives with but accepted these life-changing decisions made by their elders.

They collectively bought 200 eggs for two shillings and 13 live chickens for one shilling, in Tororo. The chickens, enclosed in a ventilated box, were addressed directly to Tek Singh in Mombasa, for collection before boarding the S.S. Karagola. They also took charcoal, wheat flour, lentils and fruit with them. Hira Singh, a tailor, who couldn't afford to pay for rations, agreed to do their cooking on the ship, in lieu of his monetary share.

Climbing up the steps to board the ship, the reality of going home struck Kartar, after having dreamt of this day for so long.

"Here I come Bebeji. I hope I have made you proud of me" was the first thought that came to his mind as he reflected on the past five years of his life in Africa. In India, he had felt like a burden on his single mother who was struggling to bring up six children. He had felt trapped in a restrictive and aimless life in the village, which had led him to run away from home twice, to join sadhus in camps of holy men at the age of fifteen, in search of some purpose in life. He had longed to be free to prove himself. After a shaky start, he felt he had finally landed on his feet and felt worthy of his mother's difficult decision to send him 3000 miles away to Africa. He had a steady income and had lived frugally in order to send money back home to support the family. The loneliness and hardship of the past five years had been compensated for by the wonderful and adventurous experience of living in the heartland of Africa. He had started eating meat with an occasional alcoholic drink, something he would not have been able to afford in India. Perhaps, a sinful act in the eyes of some judgmental people back home but it was a part of the package for Indians trying to settle and survive in Africa. He looked down with pride at his white shirt, tie, tailored Western suit and smart leather shoes. He had come a long way from the day he had first set foot in the country at the same spot, as a naive young lad wearing a kurta, a cotton suit and Indian sandals.

The boys were aware of what to expect on the journey. The ship, S.S. Karagola had similar arrangements to S.S. Alora. Their tickets were for the third-class section in open halls below deck where camp beds were available for three shillings each. Due to limited ventilation, the area tended to get very hot, so passengers tried to move to the cooler deck to sleep in the fresh air, on the covers of the luggage hatches, called falkas. After hiring their camp beds, storing the food rations and personal belongings in their place, they were ready for their journey.

The excitement of going home and having free time on the ten-day journey by ship meant mischief for young adults in their early twenties. They played tricks on fellow passengers to gain open, airy space on the ship's sultry deck, by one of them pretending to be a scary mad man. They also hatched a plot to pass Hira Singh's bundle of taxable silk cloth material through the customs, in full view of everyone. They tied the whole length of the material into a humongous, comical turban on their friend's head, taking advantage of the fact that nobody would dare question a Sikh's religious symbol. The successful execution of this plot was a badge of honor for them. Kartar, being a gripping narrator, turned these youthful pranks into the most colorful stories to narrate and boast about for a long time to come.

A three-day long journey from Bombay by steam train, brought Kartar to his hometown Khanna. As the train pulled into Khanna station, Kartar felt moved to see a big group of men from his village, waiting to welcome him. His eyes searched for his mother, but he couldn't see her. His brothers and friends took charge of his luggage as they started walking towards their village. Kartar's feet picked up pace at each step, in his eagerness to meet his mother, whom he had not seen for nearly five years. She was waiting for him just outside the village. He ran the last few yards to embrace his dear mother and they held each other in a long hug, without saying anything. The silent tears of happiness rolling down their cheeks spoke volumes of their overwhelming emotions, after such a long separation.

At home, after a few minutes of small talk, the conversation inevitably turned to Kartar's Naniji [grandmother]. Kartar couldn't stop his tears from flowing when his mother told him how much his Naniji had missed him and talked about him. Over the next few days Kartar found himself wandering around the house, gazing longingly at all the things which his Naniji had used, subconsciously hoping to find her sitting in her favorite places.

Marriage

Kartar got married to Angrez Kaur on April 4, 1932. Angrez means English, a name presumably chosen to reflect her fair complexion. The marriage party consisted of around thirty people. Kartar did not have many close relatives due to his father being an only son. His father's cousins were against the marriage, mainly due to jealousy over the family's success, so they were not invited. They spread rumors that Kartar was an old man, so the bride's uncle was sent to check out the bridegroom, en route to the wedding. No-one from the bride's side had seen Kartar prior to the wedding day, due to him being in East Africa when the wedding was settled.

The marriage party arrived in tangas [two wheeled horse drawn carts], raths [enclosed bullock drawn carts], gaddas [water-buffalo drawn open carts], horses and camels. They had a Hindu wedding ceremony, as was common in those days. Kartar looked dashing in his smart achkan suit [knee length decorated garment worn with Indian trousers]. Angrez's elder sister and cousins braided her hair and helped her to adorn her red bridal clothes and gold ornaments. The word 'make-up' did not exist in their dictionary or lives. Angrez stood smiling coyly as they all admired her radiant natural beauty, but her moment of glory was short-lived. Just before the ceremony, her mother wrapped a sheet around her, covering her from head to toe. The girls felt it was unfair but were resigned to the fact that traditions had to be followed. So, on the big day, the groom and the bride walked around the sacred fire seven times to tie the knot to spend a lifetime together, without catching a glimpse of each other's face or exchanging a single word!

Angrez was born in 1916 at Badochi Kalan, a chiefdom of Maharaja of Patiala. Her actual date of birth was never recorded. Her maiden name was Seera. She was proud of her roots, always emphasizing that Kalan meant a big village. She was the middle one of three sisters. Her only brother, Amar Singh, was the youngest. She was denied the education she craved and deserved, as there were no schools for girls in her village.

She was sixteen when she got married to twenty-year-old Kartar. She possessed a gentle nature and had led a very sheltered life before their wedding. Her only outings had been to her mother's maternal village or the annual visits to a local temple. Her uncle had served in the British Army, and for a short time was stationed in Kenya during World War I. Some familiarity with Kenya in her family might also have played a role in a marriage that would ultimately take her there.

In July, just over two months after arriving in India, Kartar left for Kenya with his bride by his side. He saw her face for the first time in full daylight on the train journey to Bombay. At the time, it was normal in villages for young brides to cover their faces during the day in the presence of men, including their husbands. On the three-day long train journey, Kartar, who was an eloquent narrator, kept the other passengers enthralled with his tales while his wife kept her head bowed as she listened in silence and smiled shyly. Having never visited a city before, Angrez looked around in awe at the hustle and bustle of Bombay, as she followed her confident husband. She marveled at the sight of the mighty Indian Ocean and the huge ship, just as her young husband had done on his maiden voyage almost five years ago.

Kartar was a seasoned traveler now, this being his third journey across the Ocean, so he explained everything with a hint of amusement, each time Angrez pointed at a new sight in wonder and excitement. His extroverted nature made the journey easier for her despite the rough, stormy weather. They got to know each other better and enjoyed the few stolen moments of private conversations, despite the lack of privacy, as men and women stayed in segregated groups on the deck. Mombasa seemed alien to her, seeing Africans for the first time in her life. The train journey from Mombasa, which never failed to captivate first time travelers, with its thrilling abundance of freely roaming wildlife, felt like an 'out of this world' experience to Angrez.

In the world that Angrez had left behind in India, women were not supposed to expose any part of their bodies except their hands and feet. They were expected to keep their heads covered with a head scarf, which could be pulled down to completely or partially cover their faces in the presence of men. Angrez's first glimpse of European women on the upper decks of the ship, freely mixing with men while wearing summer dresses which exposed their legs, arms and faces in public, must have appeared shocking to her. Now on her train journey to Nairobi, the morning sunrise brought into view an African family waving to the passing train. The mother, wearing nothing except strings of colorful beaded necklaces around her neck, stood exposing the beauty of her dark smooth skin for all to admire, without a hint of awkwardness. Angrez's world was changing fast.

Two weeks after arriving in Nairobi, Kartar's elder sister from Kisumu came to see him and his bride. On her return to Kisumu, Angrez accompanied her for a short vacation and to learn more about an Indian wife's role in Kenyan life, which differed so much from that of a wife in rural India.

On his return from India, Kartar was posted to Nairobi as a "Train clerk."

A year that had started with sickness and heartache ended in Kartar finally fulfilling his dreams of settling down with his gentle wife by his side, to set up their first home.

CHAPTER 6

1933
Married Life in Nairobi

In Nairobi, Kartar rented a single unfurnished room in a house owned by an Indian lady called Premo. The house was on a main street called Government Road. The newlyweds did not have beds or any other furniture and slept on makeshift mattresses. Two months later, they moved to married quarters near the station, allotted by the Railways. The two-bedroom house was made of wood with a corrugated metal sheet roof. There was an outside water tap and an indoor toilet with a square bucket which was emptied by sanitary services each evening via a small trap door behind the bucket. To the young couple it was luxurious accommodation.

Kartar, feeling more settled for the first time since his arrival in East Africa, bought two beds, cooking utensils, and two thaals [Indian steel plates], steel bowls and spoons. Later, he bought a china tea set consisting of a teapot and six cups and saucers. A few months later he bought four used rickety cane chairs from NM Mistry's shop on Government Road, but constantly had to tie their legs with strings to steady them, before any guests arrived. After a while, they moved into a proper bricks and mortar, two-bedroom railway accommodation on Sandiford Road, in a row of breeze block houses, each with a small enclosed backyard.

SANDIFORD ROAD RAILWAYS SPORTS CLUB, NAIROBI, 1933.
KARTAR IS SITTING IN THE MIDDLE

Misadventure on a Motorbike

Kartar bought a second hand AJS motorbike for 150 shillings from the owner of a cushion-making shop "Munsha Singh & Sons." One day, on his way home from the station, a Morris Minor overtook him soon after he had crossed over the railway lines. He wanted to race and overtake it to impress his wife and her friends who he knew would be sitting at the front of the houses, doing their usual embroidery, crocheting or knitting in the afternoon sun. He misjudged the bike's speed and the distance towards an approaching sharp left turn. The loose gravel on the unpaved road added to the problem. As he turned around the corner, the bike slipped away from under his legs and slid sideways, dragging him along for part of the way, before parting company.

A loud thump followed by the noise of metal crashing and scraping along the ground, made the ladies jump to their feet. They stood in shocked silence at the sight of the rider and his motorbike lying on the ground. The European car driver stopped his car and came to Kartar's assistance. He grabbed Kartar's outstretched arm and pulled him to his feet. The left side of Kartar's body was badly bruised and scraped, but his limbs were all in one piece. He picked up Kartar's turban from the ground and wrapped his arm around Kartar's shoulders, assisting him to limp towards the ladies. This is when Angrez realized that the crazy rider was her husband.

She rushed towards Kartar, and hurriedly covered her head with her dupatta [head scarf], before thanking the car driver with a gesture of folded hands. She nursed Kartar's wounds over the next few days. His friends brought his bike home. The accident and the money spent on an unnecessary item like a bike, at a time when the family back home was in desperate need of money, was kept a secret from his siblings and mother. Impulse buying and taking risks was part of his character, which sometimes led to bad outcomes.

Economic Depression of 1930s Hits Home

In the early 1930s, with a worsening economic outlook, the Kenyan government introduced cost saving measures. In a move to cut down on its expenses, the Railways in Kenya took away some of the benefits it offered to Indian workers, like pensions, free medical care, long leave with full pay and free passage back to India. The status of "permanent" workers was reverted to "temporary" and their wages were cut to half.

With reduced wages and higher cost of living in Nairobi, Kartar found it difficult to make ends meet and requested a transfer to the smaller rural town of Tororo where he had lived before. His request was granted and he was transferred to Tororo in June 1935.

Form No. K.U.R. 316

Memorandum Kenya and Uganda Railways and Harbours S/T. 3264
Reference No.

TRANSPORTATION DEPARTMENT DATE 15th May, 193_5_

Mr. Kartar Singh, *Clerk* Class V,
Station Master
NAKURU.

Through The Acting District Traffic Superintendent,
NAKURU.

18 MAY 1935
NAKURU

RE: DATE OF CONFIRMATION.

Your application of the 3rd instant.

The Hon. The General Manager has accorded sanction
to your confirmation being antedated to the 17th May, 1928, i.e.
the date of your first appointment in the service.

Provident Fund contribution for the period you
were previously treated as on probation, will be deducted from
your current month's salary i.e. Shs. 80/83.

STATION MASTER ACTING SUPERINTENDENT OF THE LINE.
NAKURU

A LETTER DATED MAY 15, 1935 CONFIRMING KARTAR'S JOB
STATUS AS PERMANENT, POSSIBLY IMPLYING THAT HIS EMPLOYMENT
WAS REVERTED TO PROBATION STATUS IN 1933

CHAPTER 7

1936 - 1937
Impact of World Conflicts
on East Africa

The impending war in Europe, Japanese invasions in the Far East and the Italian occupation of Ethiopia, all contributed to the disruption of lives in Kenya. Recession, high inflation, governments needing to divert resources for defense, resulted in many Indians being laid off from work or having to accept a reduction in wages. This forced them to borrow money to make ends meet.

In February 1935, Gurmukh had returned to Kenya, from India and had started working with the Railways in Nairobi. The following two letters from Gurmukh in Nairobi to Kartar in Tororo, capture the plight of Indians at the time.

Apart from their own increased expenses, the two brothers were also supporting the needs of a growing family back in India and were providing for improvements to the family home. The loan might have been taken out to pay for Gurmukh's fare back to Kenya. Neither of them had completed the final year of high school education, partly due to the family's financial situation and there is a mention of sending the third brother, Shangara, to a nearby large town for further education.

Letter from Gurmukh Singh in Nairobi (July/August 1936)

Dear brother Kartar Singh Ji,

May you have a long life, Sat Siri Akal.

I received Sh. 170 you sent with Inder Singh. I am putting aside Sh 20 for my trip to Kisumu, assuming my leave gets approved.

Regarding Vassanji's Sh 400 loan, I have already returned Sh 100 and will now pay him additional Sh 200 (by adding 50 to the 150 shillings sent by you). I will pay back the remaining Sh 100 plus interest, over the next few months.

I still owe Sh 75 to Sampuran Singh. This includes Sh 50 for last month's living expenses and Sh 12 for a trip I took to Mombasa.

There were four of us sharing our living expenses. Harbans Singh has been laid off and is looking for a cheaper place to live. Pritam Singh has gone and that leaves two of us. The other person earns Sh 385 per month and can afford to pay his half share, but I have decided to terminate this arrangement. I have found new living arrangements for Sh 60, which will leave me with savings of Sh 80 from my wages of Sh 140, after deductions. From my next month's savings, I will return 50 to Sampuran Singh and the remaining 30 to Vassanji as my next month's installment.

Now regarding the letter from home, you sent Rs 35
for work on the family house. They are now asking
for an additional Rs 30.

Apart from that let me know your thoughts regarding
Shangara Singh [younger brother] getting admission
in Ludhiana. This will be another Rs 33 plus other
school expenses on top of 100 to 120 shillings needed
for family expenses in India. I can contribute Rs 11
[20 shillings] each month and send it to Ramgarh's
address.

Perhaps this month you may not be able to send any
more money due to your still outstanding debts so
do not put yourself in any trouble. With new living
arrangements and Vassanji's debt settled, I should
be able to save 80 shillings per month. After this if a
need arises at home, then in 4 or 5 months both of
us can send our one month's salaries.

My thinking is, as you have mentioned previously,
from this or next month you continue sending 140/150
or whatever you can afford every month until you go
on leave. Please let us know without fail what your
advice is regarding Shangara Singh's admission. My
suggestion is that if he can spend a year there until
you go on leave to India, then that will be good. You
can bring him with you when you return to Kenya.
Rest is up to you, whatever you think is best. Please
write about your feelings on all these matters.

I applied for increment and a permanent status and
am enclosing their reply with this letter. It would have
helped to get an increment of Sh 15, but it is all up

to them. I will write home after receiving your reply. Whatever you decide regarding Shangara Singh will be done. Inform us of the full situation there. If I am allowed leave, then I will reach you on the morning of Sunday the 16th. Sat Siri Akal to you both and love to Kaka [Kartar's two-year-old son, Balbir Singh].

Your loving brother Gurmukh Singh.

I have forgotten the reply about increments at home so I will send it with my next letter.

The following letter reflects the deteriorating situation of a rise in cost of living, and people being laid off. Several men living with Gurmukh were unemployed and were relying on the employed ones for food and other support. These letters show community support among Indians. Pays were frozen or dropped in some cases. Kartar started work in 1928 at Sh 150 per month, but in 1935 Gurmukh's pay for a higher-level job was just Sh 140 a month. There is also discussion about purchasing more land in India. This was probably to meet the future needs of the family or a fallback provision, in case the brothers lost their jobs in Kenya. Again, they talk about improvements to the house in the village and preparations of a visit to India later in the year.

Letter from Gurmukh Singh in Nairobi (March 1937)

Dear brother Kartar Singh Ji, Sat Siri Akal.

I am enclosing the letter from India and will reply to it. I borrowed Sh 20 from Sardar Dayal Singh to send money home and have just 4 to 5 shillings remaining with me. As you suggested, in future we should accumulate our savings and send them home when we have saved 400 to 450 shillings. Let us target the end of August for our next transfer.

In the letter from India, I have been requested to send Sh 100 per month, but that is not possible.

According to the EU fund announcement, I will get Sh 140 per month. If I send Sh 100 to India, it will be difficult for me to live on just Sh 40.

Due to high unemployment in Nairobi some of our friends are homeless and without any money. They stay with us and there are never less than 5 or 6 mouths to feed. I spend nearly Sh 60 a month on meals alone. Harbans Singh, Sardar Sahib, Jagat Singh who was a fireman in Mombasa and Hardit Singh, a driver from Mombasa, are all unemployed and staying with us.

Never mind, whatever happens is for the good. I will definitely try to save 70 to 75 shillings a month. Hopefully by the end of August, you will have saved 300 and I shall try to put in 150. We will continue sending home Rs 300.

In my letter home, I have asked them to make an offer on Narayan's land, by paying Rs 250 deposit, the rest to be paid in September. The deposit can be paid from the savings in India. The expectation is that he will accept it. If he agrees then the balance can be paid with the Rs 300 money transfer at the end of August. Failing this they can arrange to buy some other land with the saved money. We need the land to build a

"Baitak" [Baitak literally was a lounge/living room, a traditional outbuilding to entertain formal guests away from the privacy of the family living quarters].

A Baitak and a water tap in the main house are necessary for our family's needs. From the money we transfer after August, the tap can be installed for Rs 100 and at least the three walls of the Baitak can be constructed with the remaining Rs 200. The rest can be completed slowly.

Although our house is fine for living, these will be a good addition. We will wait and see what transpires.

You and I should try our best so that decent living accommodation is completed by the time we get there. If we can, we should arrange to travel together. How is everything with Angrez Kaur? We are all fine here, in all respects. Give my regards to all your acquaintances and give us the news from Kisumu and about Kaka's [Balbir's] health.

Your loving brother Gurmukh Singh.

CHAPTER 8

1937
Nakuru

In 1937, Kartar bought a tricycle for his son Balbir, an expensive toy at the time, but it was a wonderful reflection of Kartar's adoration for his first born. Perhaps it was his deep-rooted desire to compensate for things he had missed out on during his own childhood. He was very good at the balancing act of fulfilling his family's needs with occasional treats, without overindulging. Kartar was always ready to work overtime in order to afford anything beyond his means. This was just a start. He dedicated his life and energy in creating a magical world for his children by teaching them to dream high and enjoy the simple pleasures of life.

On April 19, 1937, Angrez gave birth to their daughter Perminder Kaur, in the railway quarters of Nakuru. The family in India had selected a wife for Gurmukh. With the pending marriage and Angrez's first visit back home, Kartar wanted to buy his wife jewelry, to present her to friends and relatives in India at her finest. After discussing with his sister, he decided to buy it from Kisumu, where the price and selection of gold jewelry was better due to a large Indian population. On their next trip to Kisumu, he surprised Angrez by taking her to the selected shop. This was the first jewelry he had been able to afford. Feeling overwhelmed with emotion, she selected four bangles, one chain and two ear studs.

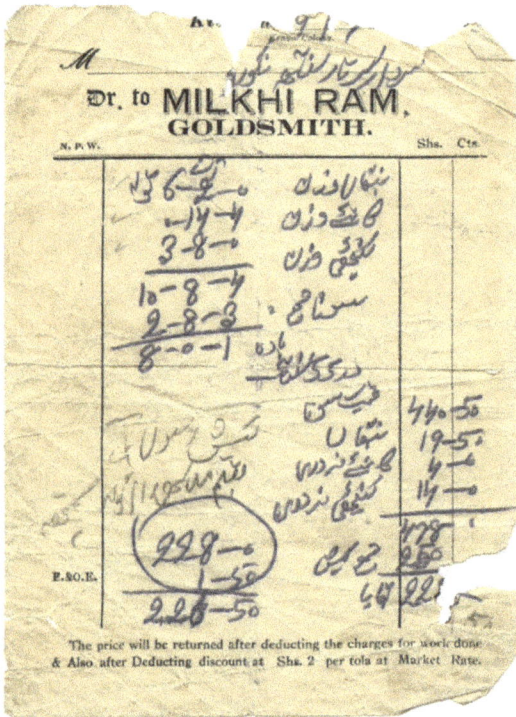

Sardar Kartar Singh Nakodar

Dr. to MILKHI RAM,

GOLDSMITH.

Bangles weight	6-2-0
Ear Rings weight	0-14-4
Pendant weight	3-8-0

Total weight	10-8-4
Impurities weight	2-8-3

Difference	8-0-1

(Note weights are in Tola-Masha-Ratti)
One Tola=11.7 grams
Price 55 rupees per tola

	Sh.	Cents
Price of gold	440	50
Bangles (labor)	19	50
Ear Rings (labor)	1	06
Pendant (labor)	14	00
---------------------	----------	----------
Total	478	06
Cash deposit	250	00
---------------------	----------	----------
Remainder	228	05
	1	50
---------------------	----------	----------
	226	50

RECEIPT FOR THE GOLD JEWELRY BOUGHT FOR ANGREZ

Second Journey Back to India

A big group of relatives decided to travel to India for Gurmukh's wedding. Gurmukh and Kartar with his family were accompanied by their sister Karam, her husband Hukam and their four children. Hukam's elder brother Kashmira Singh, his wife, his son Jagdev and daughter Sato also joined them. They left Nairobi on July 14th, landed in Bombay on July 24th and reached their village Lalheri on July 26th.

At the first stop on the train journey from Bombay to Punjab, Kartar bought datans [Neem chewing sticks] for all the children to give them their first taste of Indian life. Datans were commonly used in India to brush teeth. A short six-inch stick was first chewed at one end to expose brush-like strands which were then rubbed on the teeth. At the time children in Kenya were using toothbrushes.

By the time the traveling group reached their destination Khanna, the visitors' smart clothes were covered in soot from the steam engines of Indian trains. A group of men from the village were eagerly waiting in the rain, at Khanna train station. The villagers, mostly farmers, had brought two bullock carts for transportation of the much-awaited visitors and their luggage. As they stepped down from the train, they were warmly greeted with Sat Siri Akals [Sikh greetings] and long hugs, each hug transferring some of the soot onto the locals. The two groups were distinct in their appearance. The locals, having spent long summer days working on the farms under the hot sun, had rough, dark skin as compared to the better preserved and smooth complexions of the visitors. Over the few years in Africa, the clothing of the visitors had also evolved from that of the locals. But these outward differences were for onlookers only, because within the group, the joy of seeing each other after a long time could not tell them apart.

The luggage was loaded onto the carts. Angrez sat cross legged at the back of the cart with her baby daughter in her lap, while her son sat with the other children, dangling his legs off the rear end of the cart, enjoying the novelty of the exciting ride. The men followed on foot, on the muddy road to the village, two miles away. Kartar's mother was waiting just outside the village. She was overjoyed to see her two sons and daughter, with their families. She doted on her grandchildren and made the most of their short stays with her.

Gurmukh got married in August at his wife's village, Mangewal. The two brothers hired three horse-driven tangas to get there, which was a big expense at the time, but they could afford it and felt the need to display their financial stability. They reached Mangewal in the evening, the wedding was the next day and they returned home on the third day, as was the norm in those days.

The wedding party included their brother-in-law Hukam and his two brothers and a friend Sampuran Singh from Kenya. To impress the locals, they all dressed in Western attire. Kartar had a new pair of shoes made in Nakuru to wear at his brother's wedding, but they had shrunk a bit and felt very tight. To his embarrassment, he had to take them off and hold them in his hand as he walked barefoot next to the bridegroom on the wedding day. The two brothers wore braces, which added to the amusement of the villagers who assumed that they were wearing waist belts over their shoulders!

BEBEJI WITH HER FAMILY 1937 (PICTURE TAKEN AFTER GURMUKH'S WEDDING)
STANDING : GURMUKH S, SHANGARA S, GURDIAL S, KARTAR S
SITTING GURBACHAN K, KARTAR K, BEBEJI, KARAM K, ANGREZ K
STANDING LEFT: GURMIT S RIGHT: BALBIR S
ON FLOOR: SURJIT K, BALJIT K AND HARPAL K IN
LAP: LEFT PERMINDER K AND RIGHT BALJIT S

Gurmukh, due to his short service, only qualified for a month's leave so he left for Kenya with his wife Gurbachan Kaur, shortly after the wedding, on August 11, 1937. On his return, he was posted to Kampala as a yard foreman.

For the first few weeks, Angrez was busy with her brother-in-law's wedding and did not get a chance to visit her family. Soon after the wedding, her brother Amar came to take her to their family home. After being dropped at Khanna station by Wazir, in a gadda [bullock cart], they caught a train to Sirhind. Carrying Angrez's baby girl and toddler son in turns, they walked the last two miles to their village Badochi.

KARTAR AND ANGREZ, 1937

Angrez, who had never spent a day apart from her family before her marriage, had sorely missed her parents and siblings during her five years of separation. Although her husband wrote letters on her behalf, she had missed the personal connection with her family, not being able to write to express her true feelings of sadness and homesickness. She had felt totally cut off from her parents and siblings, around whom her small world had revolved before her marriage. With a flood of tears running down her cheeks, she gave long hugs to her parents and two sisters. Her elder sister and her two little boys had come from their village nearby. Her younger sister, who was a child when Angrez got married, peeped shyly from behind their mother, at her idolized sister, about whose new life she had heard so much. Looking at her teenage brother, standing next to their father who was in his forties, Angrez remarked how similar the two tall, handsome men looked.

With the initial emotional greetings out of the way, they all sat down cross legged on low stools to eat, while their mother cooked hot chapatis to go round. They all chatted non-stop, eager to hear all about Angrez's journey and life in Africa, which was like another planet to them. No-one from their village had ever ventured abroad, so they were full of questions, barely giving Angrez a chance to eat or reply at length.

Afterwards, during a quiet moment, Angrez looked around the house she had grown up in and had missed so much. It was a small, modest, flat roofed single story mud building, in the center of the village. It consisted of one long room, with a kitchen at the front end, and farm animals like buffaloes tied up at the rear. The outside and inside walls had been freshly lapped with cow dung for Angrez's visit.

Her parents were gentle people, with simple farming lives but big hearts full of love for her. They wanted to make the most of Angrez's short stay and couldn't get enough of their two grandchildren. There was no electricity connection or electric fans in the house, so Angrez's father would stay up late into the night, to keep his grandchildren cool as they slept, with a hand-held fan.

After Gurmukh's departure for Kenya, their mother arranged the marriage of their younger brother Shangara, to Jaswant Kaur from Rattanheri. Shangara decided to go to Kenya with Kartar and his family, so at the end of November, they left for Bombay to catch a ship to Mombasa. Shangara's bride Jaswant stayed behind, with plans to join him later. On boarding the ship, they had a medical inspection. Shangara had a small boil on his arm, which caused concern due to the possibility of plague, so he was asked to leave the ship. The two brothers scrambled to find his luggage which had already been loaded onto the ship by cranes. He ended up traveling on the next ship with Kashmira Singh, their brother-in-law Hukam's brother.

CHAPTER 9

1938
Voi, Eldoret

Life with Animals in the African Savanna

Kartar arrived back in Kenya with his family on December 4, 1937. He resumed his duties as a train clerk in Voi, which was a very small town, on the dusty unpaved road connecting Mombasa and Nairobi. Apart from being a convenient halfway point between the two major towns, it was the start of a sideline going to Taveta, on the border with Tanganyika, near Arusha and Moshi. It was built in 1912 to reach the border of German East Africa, more for security reasons than trade.

It had a gas station and a handful of dukas [shops], mainly owned and run by Gujaratis. There was a row of four houses behind the station for Indian railway employees. Kartar and his family lived in one of them. A dozen or so buildings sparsely spread out in the middle of the African savanna which was full of wild animals, made close encounters with them inevitable.

Soon after the new year, Kartar and the assistant station master were on night duty at Voi station, which consisted of just a single room. Kenya had a single rail track system, splitting into multitracks at train stations. Kartar walked out onto the platform at 2.30 am, knowing that the train from Mombasa, driven by Abdul Rehman, would be arriving soon. The signals on the entry and exit sides of the station were manually operated by wires connected to levers in a small shed on the platform. Kartar could see the lights at the front of the engine in the far distance. Out of the corner of his eye, he saw the station master, D.N. Desai, approaching from his house a few yards from the platform. As Kartar turned around, he found himself staring into four large shiny eyes looking straight at him. He waved frantically, shouting "Lions" as he rushed to the station building. Desai, who had helped Kartar to get his first job with the Railways in Jinja, quickly turned around and ran back to the safety of his house.

Kartar and the assistant station master hurriedly sent telegrams to stations on either side of the track to warn the trains about lions on the platform but could not reach the driver of the approaching train. In the still night, they could hear the engine whistles as they contemplated their next move. Kartar tied two kerosine signal lamps displaying green lights onto two broomsticks, before cautiously opening a tiny slit in the window, just enough to wave the lamps up and down. As the train slowly moved into the station, the lions, disturbed by the noise, walked away nonchalantly into the jungles, totally unaware of the drama they had caused.

One early morning, towards the end of his night shift, the sound of barking dogs alerted Kartar to the presence of animals in the vicinity. He peeped out of the rear window of the station building and saw a herd of elephants passing by. He waited for them to pass before stepping out and noticed a dark gray bundle lying on the grass. From a distance, it looked like a railway worker's winter coat, but as he approached it, he soon realized that it was a new-born baby elephant. He stroked it gently and it moved a little. It was alive! They were required to cut the tails of any elephants or giraffes found dead on railway property, following which, the DNR [Department of Natural Resources] would come and collect the animal in order to investigate the cause of death. Kartar had just sat down to write a report about the baby elephant needing help, when he heard the elephants returning. After they had passed, he stepped out to witness a heart melting scene. The whole herd was standing quietly around the baby elephant, as if they were lovingly encouraging it, because it soon got up slowly on its legs and started walking gingerly towards its mother.

In April, after a malaria attack, Kartar was transferred to Eldoret as assistant Goods Clerk. In the same month, his younger brother Shangara started work in Kampala, as an electrician for "Dharam Singh Electrical Contractors."

CHAPTER 10

1939
Life in Eldoret

A Web of Love, Violent Abuse and Horrendous Murder

Prem Singh, in his late forties, looked old for his age. His big stature and bulging stomach were well suited to his job as an "Overseer" with the Railways. An artisan by caste, he was on friendly terms with Kartar and his Jat [farmer] Sikh friends Naginder, Natha and Harnam.

Prem's marriage to a much younger Muslim girl, who had converted to Sikhism and taken a Sikh name Gian Kaur, was the talk of the town, and the general rumor was that he had purchased his wife. At the time, it was not uncommon for Indian men to buy younger wives in India. She had believed that moving overseas would hide the circumstances of their marriage, but after a decade in Eldoret, she still felt isolated from the other Indian house-wives although their two little girls and a boy enjoyed the happy Kenyan-Indian lifestyle of this small town. It was a turbulent marriage due to Prem's drinking and abusive habits. Prem's only sibling, a widowed sister, lived in India. A few years back, to help his sister, Prem had arranged for her son Mota's migration to Kenya and had found him a job locally. Mota started volunteering as a librarian with the "Railway Institute" where Kartar was a treasurer, so they became good friends.

Prem's job would take him away from home for days, to visit local towns. He accused his nephew Mota of fooling around with his wife in his absence, and the arguments between the three got worse. One evening, after a meeting at the Railway Institute, Mota's uncle Niranjan asked Kartar to dissuade Mota from taking a rash step like trying to get rid of his uncle Prem. Next evening, Kartar took Mota for a walk around the playing fields adjoining the library. He spoke about the consequences of his actions and the impact it would have on his old mother in India who depended on his financial support. Kartar advised him to go and live with his cousin in Kampala and start a new life there. Mota seemed lost in his thoughts and departed with the comment "I do not intend to do anything of the sort. It was said in the heat of the moment." Not wanting to stir an already troubled relationship, Kartar kept the conversation of the evening to himself.

A few weeks later, a blood-stained sack containing Prem's remains was found lying in the grass near the Railway Club, by an early morning walker. People started gathering around it and as soon as Gian stepped out of her house, she was bombarded with questions. She ranted and raved about her husband's murder and blamed his upright Jat Sikh friends, who she claimed were jealous of a non-jat rising to the position of an Overseer. When Mota joined the crowd, someone noticed and pointed out a blood stain on his turban. He slipped away quietly to avoid any commotion, but a police inspector who had witnessed this, followed Mota, and caught him red handed, trying to wash off the blood stain and arrested him.

The news of the murder spread quickly around the neighbourhood. When Kartar came out to investigate further, he met police inspector Lal Chand Syal, a good friend of his, who advised Kartar not to go anywhere near the scene as Gian was accusing Prem's Jat friends, Naginder, Natha, Harnam and Kartar. Mota and Gian were both interrogated and arrested. The time before and during the trial was a very difficult and stressful period for Kartar and his three friends as they feared that Gian would implicate them somehow. Kartar lost his appetite and had difficulty sleeping or concentrating during that dark period of uncertainty.

A few months later, while Kartar was walking along the platform with police inspector Lal Chand, an askari [African policeman] requested them to accompany him to a coach waiting on the second platform line. These coaches waited at Eldoret, to be attached to the Kampala to Nairobi train, when it arrived at noon. On entering the compartment, they saw a hand-cuffed Mota sitting with a police sub-inspector and an askari on either side. They were escorting him to the prison in Nairobi, to be hanged in two days' time. Struggling to hold back his tears, Mota unburdened himself and said he needed to lighten the load of his guilt before being hanged. This is when Kartar learnt the full details of Mota's actions on that dreadful day.

Mota confessed everything and said he should have followed Kartar's advice, but he just couldn't leave Gian on her own, to face a lifetime of violence and degradation. He said Gian was treated like a slave and suffered from physical and mental abuse most evenings after Prem's heavy drinking sessions with his mates. Mota said his heart wept for this lonely girl with no family or friends. Gian, seeking a shoulder to cry on, was drawn towards Mota, who was always kind and protective towards her. Their relationship deepened and became intimate, and rumors of their love spread around the town. Fueled by these rumors, Prem's ill treatment of Gian became unbearable. That was when Mota and Gian hatched a plan to murder Prem.

Late one afternoon Mota invited their domestic help Katoshi and his brother over for drinks and shared his plan with them, offering money for their assistance. Prem arrived home late and ended the day with his usual drunken abuse. Mota waited for Prem to fall asleep before entering the room stealthily and on hearing the snoring, signaled to the others to enter. Mota and Katoshi took their position on either side, Gian towards the head and Katoshi's brother at the foot of the bed. Mota stabbed Prem in the chest with a knife. As Prem sat up in shock, Mota and Katoshi stabbed a few more times, until the body lay still. Finally, Gian took the knife from Katoshi and put all her pent-up fears and rage into one last slash, to behead Prem. The three men stuffed the remains of Prem in a large hessian sack. While carrying it towards the local woods, they saw someone in the grounds of the Railway Club. They panicked, dropped the sack, and ran away. Mota gave the two Africans 200 shillings and Prem's expensive watch, before they fled to their village near Kitale. Prem and Gian cleaned up all evidence and disposed of the bedding.

The trial started a few months later and lasted a few weeks. Mota was represented by Gautam who practiced both in Nairobi and Eldoret. Gian's lawyer was Shaw, an English attorney. Mota's defense was that during a heated argument, Prem had tried to stab him, but he had snatched the knife and stabbed Prem in self-defense. The children were questioned and the key prosecution witness in the trial was their ten-year-old daughter. Her detailed testimony was presented in the court. Noise of the stabbing had woken her up and she had witnessed the body being placed in the sack.

Mota was found guilty of murder and was sentenced to death by hanging. Gian was charged as an accessory in murder, and was given a suspended sentence, considering her violent, abusive marriage and her young children, who needed her care.

World War Brings an Opportunity for Promotion

In September 1939, when war was declared, Italians and Germans were rounded up. In Eldoret, a grocery shop called "Rogers and Co." owned by a German family was shut down and the owners were arrested. Several Italian farmers from the surrounding areas were also arrested, and an open area near Kartar's house was converted to an "Army prison camp".

In anticipation of war, the goods traffic in Kenya increased significantly. Trains to the coast carried produce like sugar, cotton and coffee from Kenya and Uganda, for export to England. The first sugar mill in Kenya, the Victoria Nyanza Sugar Company, was a direct result of the Asian commercial cane farming in the Kibos-Muhoroni area. Returning trains were loaded with military and other defense needs, including petrol. This put a big strain on yard foremen who were responsible for logistics of arranging and rearranging the train bogies for different destinations. Fearing the imminent war, some Indian yard foremen left for India, which exacerbated the situation further. This was across all railway junctions in East Africa but the situation in Nairobi was most critical, being the main hub in Kenya.

There was a drive to recruit many new yard foremen in the three East African countries. In December, as part of this drive, the 'Operating Superintendent of Railways' visited all major train stations including Eldoret. Getting wind of this news, Kartar approached the station master, Ramlal Bowrey for a recommendation. He felt he was in the right place at the right time and didn't want to miss this opportunity. Yard foreman's job was hard work but came with higher wages that Kartar desperately needed for his growing family. He sent off his application and was called for an interview. With a glowing recommendation from Ramlal, Kartar was promoted to a yard foreman, based in Nairobi. The promotion came with a pay rise to 240 shillings per month.

The year 1939 brought big family changes for Kartar. His son Balbir started school on September 5th. His brother Shangara's wife arrived from India. Kartar and Shangara went to pick her up from Mombasa. The couple spent a few days with Kartar and his family in Eldoret, before proceeding to Kampala. On December 14th, Kartar's third child, a son, Harcharan was born.

CHAPTER 11

1940
Nairobi

Disastrous Split-Second Decisions

Kartar started his job as a yard foreman in Nairobi on 9th May. Running back and forth along with the bogies as they were moved from one train to another and jumping over tracks with a red and green flag, was physically hard work. The points to divert the trains at a junction were operated by a points-man, under directions from the foreman. Under the segregated jobs system, all points-men and a few shunting engine drivers were Africans. Kartar had joined a number of new recruits like Sucha Singh, Basant Singh and Pritam Singh. They were all Jat Sikhs, making it evident that the English superintendent preferred Jat Sikhs for the job. Having descended from physically hard-working farming families, in his mind they were better suited for the job, and they proved him right over the next few years.

With war efforts in full swing, a POW camp was built in Nairobi, near the present-day Remand Prison at the junction of Enterprise Road and Athi River Road. It was for Italians captured in the Abyssinian War (October 1935 to February 1937).

On a Sunday morning, Kartar's boss, the yardmaster, approached him with a request to guide the delivery of two bogies of rations to the POW camp. With the help of a shunting engine and its African driver and two African points-men, Mangi and Jugana (from the Kikuyu tribe), they moved two bogies to the loading platform inside the POW camp. Both perishable and non-perishable food was quickly off loaded before starting their return journey with the two empty bogies plus two others that had been left from a previous delivery.

The sun was setting when the train approached the crossing over the road connecting Unga Limited to Enterprise Road, slowing down to let the two points-men get down to stop the car traffic. But the points-men said it was getting late and asked for this precaution to be skipped as the roads were traffic free, it being a Sunday evening. Seeing that the road was clear, Kartar reluctantly agreed, and they proceeded. As the first bogie went over the road, a military Land Rover came round the corner at high speed and hit the slow-moving bogie. The vehicle got dragged a few feet with its left side pushed against the side of the bogie. There were four occupants in the car, two African soldiers and two British officers. Everyone on the train rushed to help the occupants. One African soldier on the back seat had no pulse and the second one ran away in panic. The British officer, Captain Crawford in the front passenger seat had blood trickling from his mouth and was badly injured with head wounds. The driver, British officer Major Matthew, seemed to have escaped with minor injuries and a broken arm.

While everyone was trying to tend to the injured, the Major started shouting at Kartar, accusing him for not manning the crossing and even threatened to shoot him. Kartar apologized profusely for his mistake while reminding him of the urgency to get to a hospital. The Major calmed down and suggested that they should go to Command General Hospital. Kartar gave him his thermos of hot coffee and ran towards the Unga Limited factory, which he knew was open on Sundays and had a phone on site. He suspected that his three African companions would be barred from entry or use of a phone because of their skin color. Kartar was met by the supervisor, Daljeet, who he knew as the brother of a railway guard, Ram.

Kartar dialed the number and explained the urgency of the situation to the emergency services. The ambulances arrived soon after and took away the two officers and the dead body. Kartar accompanied them to the hospital, where the captain's condition deteriorated and he passed away half an hour later. Kartar sat down, feeling shocked and stunned as the gravity of the situation hit him. He was full of remorse for the suffering caused by a split second of a wrong decision on his part. The anguish on Kartar's face as he waited for Matthew to come out of the operation theater, drew a uniformed gentleman to enquire after his wellbeing. He consoled Kartar and offered to arrange for him to be taken to the railway station, but Kartar refused to leave until Matthew's wellbeing was confirmed.

Finally, when Kartar arrived at the station, Mr. Bishop, who was in charge of the yard, a few ranks above Kartar, was waiting for him.

He said, "It is late at night, and you have been through enough for one evening, so go home and rest. Write a detailed report about the incident first thing in the morning. I have already dispatched a summary of what I know."

Next Morning, a very shaken Kartar got to work early and started writing his report, which took several attempts. His boss made some suggestions for clarification, and the process was repeated a few times until the report was finalized and ready to be sent to bosses up the ladder. While writing, Kartar was advised by others to cover up some of the details in order to save his job. Kartar said he had caused enough pain and needed to face the consequences of his decision. He stuck to the truth when he wrote in his defense that they were already running late and it was a joint decision, but he accepted the responsibility, being the person in charge. He also included a short conversation he had with Matthew on the way to the hospital, who had said, "Don't blame yourself. It was my mistake too. I turned the corner very fast, and on seeing the train, my first reaction was to floor the paddle to beat the train. It all happened in a split second and by the time I decided to brake, it was too late. The next thing I heard was a loud noise of metal grating against metal. I will help you if I can."

There were two inquiries, one by a Railway team and the other by the Military board. Kartar participated in both. The first was with a large group of participants and the second one was with a panel of military personnel. A few months went by without any news, which caused Kartar a lot of worry. He was constantly bombarded by thoughts of losing his job or even the possibility of a jail sentence and worried about how his family would cope with it. Thoughtless remarks by some unkind associates, like "how long before you leave" or calling him "a temporary worker" did not help the situation.

One evening around four, just as Kartar was packing up to go home, his boss Mr. Drummond signaled him to come to his office. His clerk Faquir Balota, an Indian, was also there. Kartar could sense it was bad news, when Mr Drummond greeted him with a stern face and said, "We have received your arrest warrant and the military police will be here soon. If you wish to send a message home, Mr. Balota will deliver it for you."

Kartar replied "Please ask my wife not to worry and stay with the children. Give them the address where they can come and visit me in the morning."

With that, Mr. Drummond started laughing and said that there would be no charges against him. Failure to deploy points-men to man the crossing was not the main factor causing the accident. The positive report from the Military Head Office continued to thank Kartar for his quick reaction in calling the emergency services, for staying calm while comforting the injured and showing his sincere concern for them in the hospital. Major Matthew was very impressed by the way Kartar had acted, and concurred with these observations. Kartar understood that the speed of the Land Rover was the major contributing factor for the accident, which a points-man waving a flag could not have prevented. Matthew's positive and favorable statements had helped his case too. What a relief it was for Kartar and his family, when the gray cloud that had hung over his head for months was finally lifted. The immense relief was tinged with a lingering sadness for the loss of two lives.

A few weeks later, Kartar got a similar letter from the Railway headquarters, confirming the outcome and thanking Kartar for acting responsibly by taking the injured men to the hospital, and not leaving until he was satisfied that Major Matthew was okay. Mr. Drummond was relieved and praised Kartar for his handling of the situation, his hard work and work performance. He recommended Kartar for promotion to grade 1010, a Senior Yard foreman with a salary increase to three hundred and fifty shillings per month and entitlement to second class travel on trains and ships. This was Kartar's promotion to the highest grade for a yard foreman, which came with supervisory responsibilities of junior yard foremen. One of the requirements for the promotion was knowledge of the local language, Swahili.

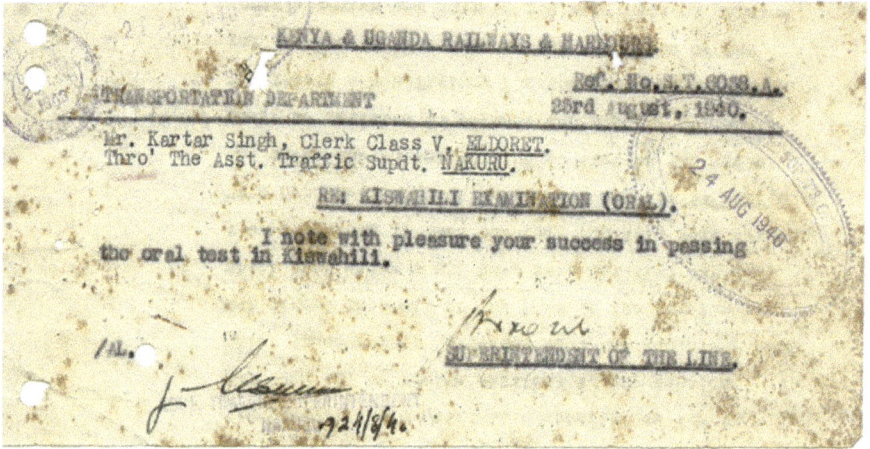

KENYA & UGANDA RAILWAYS & HARBOURS

TRANSPORTATION DEPARTMENT

Ref. No. S.T.6038.A.
23rd August, 1940.

Mr. Kartar Singh, Clerk Class V, ELDORET.
Thro' The Asst. Traffic Supdt. NAKURU.

RE: KISWAHILI EXAMINATION (ORAL).

I note with pleasure your success in passing the oral test in Kiswahili.

SUPERINTENDENT OF THE LINE.

KARTAR'S SWAHILI CERTIFICATE

CHAPTER 12

1942
Family Reunion in India

KARTAR & ANGREZ WITH THEIR SONS BALBIR, HARCHARAN, AND
DAUGHTER PERMINDER, NAIROBI. CIRCA EARLY 1941

Hurdles in Getting Leave and Passage During Wartime

All of Kartar's brothers were married and were now in India, with their families. He had not seen some of the new additions to the family and longed to be with his mother and everyone else. Providing food and other necessities for the war in Europe was the top priority so all leave for essential government employees in Kenya was canceled. Railway workers were included in this category as they were responsible for moving supplies. It became difficult for Kartar to get approval for his entitled long leave of four months, after every five years of service. It was five years since Kartar's last leave in 1937, and he was due for one. Due to the war, leave was only granted for family emergencies or on medical recommendations by a doctor.

He needed to find a way around these restrictions. He had always suffered from severe migraine attacks, which necessitated sick leave sometimes. Whenever Kartar had bad migraine episodes, he would visit Dr. Sargent, who was the family doctor for Indian railway workers. He had his office in a wooden building opposite the Norfolk Hotel [at the site of present-day University of Nairobi]. Being on friendly terms with the doctor, Kartar approached him for a recommendation for leave, to recover from his stress-related headaches. Kartar's argument was that a long leave for full recovery would result in fewer sick days on his return.

"I can recommend a leave for some days so you can go to Mombasa for a rest" said Dr. Sargent.

Kartar replied with a charming smile "Perhaps a little longer?"

Having worked with Indians, the doctor could see right through Kartar's charm!

"If I am not mistaken, going to India will provide the only magic cure" he replied with a knowing smile.

"Yes, I have not seen my family for five years and am longing to be with them" Kartar implored.

"I will make a recommendation; the rest depends on the railway bureaucrats. Good luck in getting tickets for the ship journey" added the doctor.

Kartar thanked him and left. A few days later he got a letter saying that his leave for 100 days had been approved. There was a condition attached to the approval that on arrival in Bombay, a medical board would examine him. Kartar never understood the reason for a medical test for migraine but had the wisdom not to question it.

The next step was to get permission to leave the country. Under a new law introduced in 1942 restrictions were placed on Indians leaving Kenya.

EXIT PERMITS

GOVERNMENT NOTICE NO. 256 OF 1942

IN EXERCISE of the powers conferred upon him by Regulation 27 of the Defence Regulations, 1939, His Excellency the Governor has been pleased to order as follows with effect from the 23rd of March, 1942 : —

1. No person shall proceed from the Colony to a destination outside the Colony except under the authority of a written permit granted by the Commissioner of Police or by any person authorized by the Commissioner of Police in that behalf.

2. The Commissioner of Police shall, before issuing a permit to any person, consult the Director of Man Power as to the desirability or otherwise of granting a permit to such person.

Luckily for Kartar, the above law had just been put into practice and the full process was not in place yet. Also, the recommendation letter from the railways helped him to obtain the 'Exit Permit' which was stamped in his passport.

With time this 'Exit Permit' became difficult to obtain as most of the applications were rejected by the 'Director of Man Power'. This became a major source of discontent among Indians, resulting in the assassination of the Deputy Director of Indian Man Power, Isher Dass by two Indians. He was assassinated in his office in Desai Memorial Hall building.

The next hurdle was to get tickets for the ship journey to India. Most of the passenger services between Kenya and India were being utilized for transportation of troops. The inability to get tickets on the regular route to India, led some desperate people to use alternative routes and means. One such route was to get to Aden via the River Nile, and then by ship to India. It was easier to get a passage to India from Aden, due to heavy traffic between Europe and the Far East, with a stopover in Aden and Bombay.

Kartar's good friend, Pyarelal Sharma had used this route. The other option was to travel on dhows but both options were rough and difficult, especially with young children.

Kartar's friend Swaran, who was recovering from a heart attack, was also granted leave to recuperate and had decided to go to India. In the BI [British India Steam Navigation Company] office in Mombasa, Swaran and Kartar pleaded their case based on their health conditions and their need for recuperation in the comfort of their village environments. Both were given special approval by the medical board, to travel with their families. They got tickets for S.S. Karagola sailing from Mombasa on June 27th.

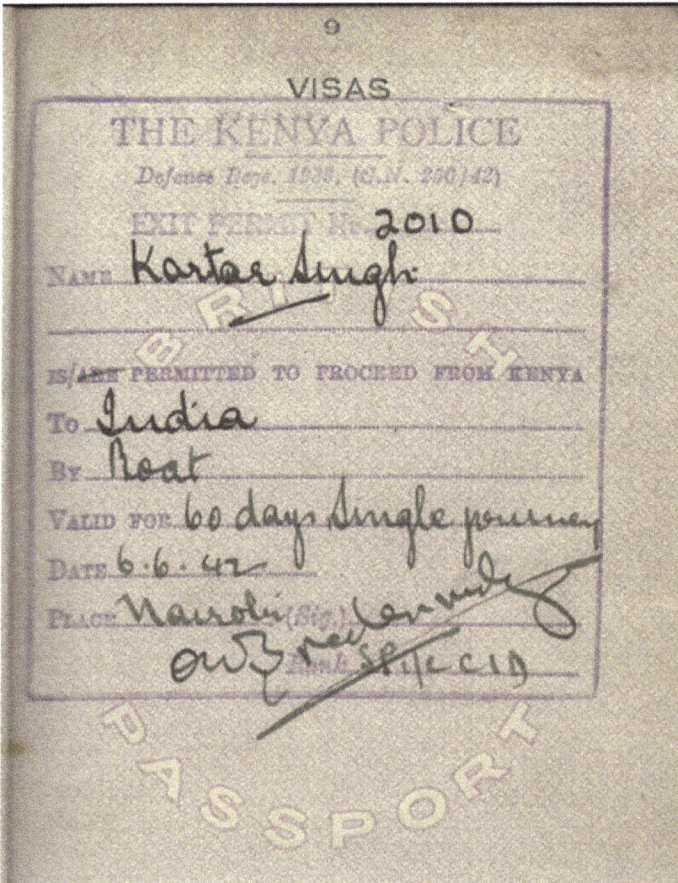

EXIT PERMIT STAMPED IN KARTAR'S PASSPORT

Ship Journey to India

As the tugboats slowly pulled the ship away from the harbor, the cool, rejuvenating evening breeze was a welcome change from the hectic formalities of boarding the ship in the heat of the afternoon sun. The passengers stood behind the rails, watching the people, cranes and a few vehicles on the harbor slowly fading away into the distance.

Kartar felt very excited at the prospect of meeting his family, especially his mother. His wife Angrez's excitement was overshadowed by her sadness, as she knew that the two persons she had missed the most, would not be there to welcome her back. Both her parents had passed away since her last trip five years ago. Although she looked forward to meeting her siblings and their families, she could not shift the deep feeling of dread at how her birthplace and home would feel in the absence of the warm essence of her loving parents. They both looked forward to seeing the new additions to the extended family and to proudly introduce their four children to family and friends back home.

Kartar's six-month-old boy Balwinder was an adorable and chubby baby, always happy and smiling. European ladies from the upper decks would come down to hold him. One of them got very attached to the baby and would often ask for their permission to take him upstairs to the first and second-class areas.

Unexpected Break in the Journey, on an Exotic Island

A few days after being on the sea, a crackly voice on the speakers announced that a Japanese submarine had sunk an Australian ship in the Indian Ocean, so their ship would go to the port of Seychelles for safety, to await further instructions after full assessment of the situation. Despite feeling a bit concerned, the passengers carried on enjoying their daily routine. The following morning, on July 11th, they reached the port of Seychelles which was only accessible via boat.

The ship's captain decided to let the passengers visit the island and arranged for boats to take them ashore. Kartar jumped at the opportunity for an adventure and landed on the island with his family. He was surprised to see a lot of Sikhs, who were part of the British army, stationed on the Island.

From the landing jetty, a wide dirt road led up to the hilltop. The steep climb was slow, but it gave them the perfect opportunity to browse through the local goods on display along the roadside. They were fascinated by the size of the seashells and giant turtles and bought some seashells.

Halfway up the hill was a big hall that had been converted to a temporary Sikh temple, where the preparations for the celebration of Gurpurab, a Sikh holy day were in full swing. Indian food according to Sikh traditions was being served. Kartar and his family joined in and sat cross legged on mats laid out in rows, reminding them of visits to their Gurudwara in Nairobi.

After lunch, army trucks took them on a tour of the Mahe Island [the main island of Seychelles]. The rocky trails and lush greenery with a splendid view of the sea around every corner, brought loud exclamations of 'aahs' and 'oohs' from the passengers. The bumpy ride bounced the tightly packed riders in unison up in the air and jolted them against each other. They saw giant turtles in their natural, wild habitat. They came across occasional huts, with merchandise displayed outside for sale, like seashells of various sizes, and artistic carvings from coconut shells and palm tree trunks.

On the way back they stopped once again at the Sikh Gurudwara. A holy man wearing white clothes, in sharp contrast to his long jet-black beard and bright red turban, was chanting from the holy book placed on a high platform. Another man stood behind him waving the traditional chaury sahib [Sikh flywhisk] in a rhythmic motion consistent with the chanting, occasionally shifting the whisk from one tired hand to another. After bowing down to pay their respects to the holy book, and offering money, the visiting passengers sat down cross-legged, ladies on one side and gents on the other. The book reading was followed by hymns sung by three men accompanied by a harmonium, tablas and other Indian percussion instruments. A couple of passengers from the ship joined the singing group.

After having langar, the traditional meal, most passengers went back to the ship as it was getting dark but Kartar, his family and some other Sikh passengers stayed behind to spend the night with the British Sikh soldiers. Blankets were provided in the big hall while others were given folding beds to sleep in tents outside. The next morning, just after breakfast, orders came to return to the ship, to await instructions to resume the journey. They spent the day in readiness on the ship, which finally put to sea at dawn, on July 13th. Everyone stood by the rails, watching the magical island fading away into the distance. They locked away the special memories in their hearts as a cherished dream, knowing that they would never be able to afford the luxury of another visit.

Arrival in Bombay

On landing at Bombay, Kartar reported to the medical board office at the port. He was examined by Dr. Ricky. After some basic tests, he was given a list of recommended foods and those to avoid. The list appeared to be relevant for Europeans only as most of the things on the avoid list were not available to him in his village anyway. Some exercises were recommended. He was also asked to send a health report to them in six weeks. Kartar thanked him and left the office, shaking his head in disbelief at this totally unnecessary and wasteful bureaucratic procedure. There was no room for such thoughts to linger as he walked away with a spring in his steps, each step taking him closer to his mother and siblings. He walked with his head held high, with a feeling of belonging, on the soil of his homeland, which he had missed so much in the last five years. It was a moment filled with gratitude at having his and his mother's dreams fulfilled.

A three-day train journey took Kartar's family to their home village of Lalheri where a big celebration was waiting for them. It was the first time in five years that all the siblings were together.

It was also time for Kartar's mother Bebeji to enjoy the company of her offspring, their spouses and her grandchildren, not knowing that this would be the last time she would see them all together. Her six children were all married off and settled in their lives. Her struggles and responsibilities were over. Her cherished nest, which had started to feel empty after the emigration of her three sons and their families, was once again filled with the chatter and laughter of all her family gathered under one roof. The joy of watching her fifteen grandchildren playing and running around, made her forget every sacrifice she had been forced to make during the course of her life.

Bebeji, a Cherished Mother

Sixty-year-old Bebeji's tanned skin reflected years of hard work outdoors in the sun. Her petite frame and a strong expressionless face concealed the endless struggles she had endured as an impoverished single mother raising a family in the patriarchal society of those times. The story of her lifetime was etched in the skin of her face, a smooth fair complexion from the early privileged years of married life now interspersed with wrinkles and worry lines from the stresses of the past two decades.

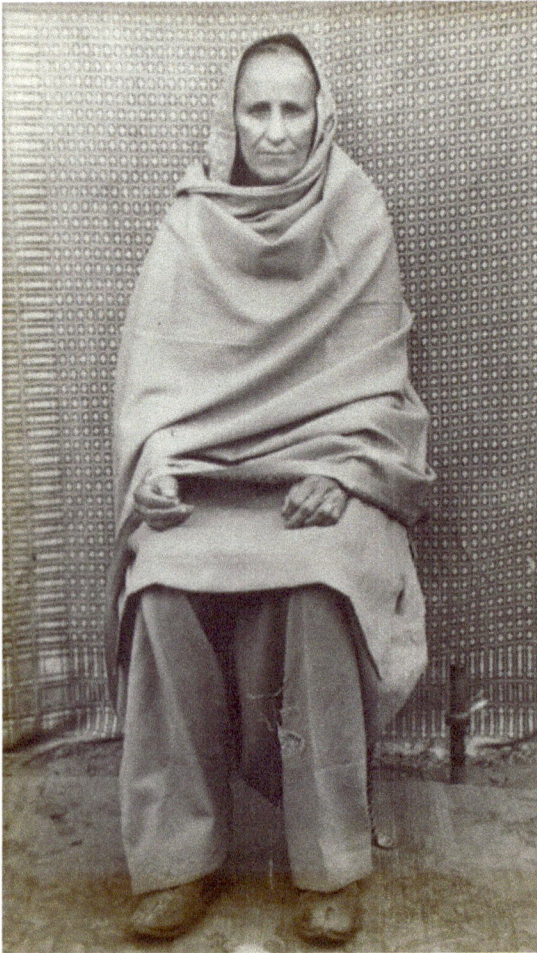

KARTAR'S MOTHER, BEBEJI, LALHERI, INDIA, 1942

72

Bebeji, Wasan Kaur, known as Basso to everyone, was born into a middle-class Punjabi family in Jago Hallotali, a small village near Patiala, under the rule of the Maharaja of Patiala. Her father, Kharor Singh Bagri was a farmer and her mother Raj Kaur Bagri, a typical village housewife. Besides the usual household chores, a farmer's wife had to help with milking and caring for farm animals, cutting and preparing their fodder and cooking and carrying food in bulk to feed all the farm workers, especially during the busy sowing and harvesting seasons.

The first sixteen years of Bebeji's life were spent with her two sisters, Rupa and Nand and brother Hazara. Rupa was the oldest, followed by Basso and then came the two younger ones. The siblings enjoyed the carefree and simple village life during their early years. Most young boys at the time had basic schooling, after which the father usually took them under his wing to teach them farming procedures. Formal education for girls was discouraged by society norms, as girls were expected to follow in their mother's footsteps. The main purpose in their life was deemed to be a dutiful wife and a good mother, roles which did not necessitate the requirement for education.

Bebeji was saved from the drudgery of a farming life, when she married twenty-seven-year-old Sham Singh, an educated young man, who held a well-paid job as a Patwari, a respected position for an Indian to hold during the British Raj. The inheritance of his father's farmland as an only child, was a very attractive consideration for farming families while selecting a marriage partner. It was an arranged marriage, but 16-year-old Bebeji's youthful fair complexion, good looks, intelligence and gentle nature soon won Sham's heart.

Marriage took her from a simple village life to that of a government officer's wife in the suburbs of the large sprawling city of Faisalabad in present day Pakistan, 160 miles away from her village. A large brick house provided by the government, with domestic help to take care of her needs, was a big change from her mud house in the village. Having lost his mother at a very young age, Sham had always craved love and attention, especially since his father did not have much time for him. Sham finally had someone by his side who gave him the love, care and companionship that he had searched for during most of his growing years. He was a devoted husband and showered his wife with expensive gifts and gold jewelry. Basso felt grateful for the comfortable life and expensive gifts but kept her feet firmly on the ground and continued to value the simple joys of family life.

Over the next fourteen years Basso accompanied her husband on his various assignments in five different places and bore him six children, four boys and two girls. Kartar was fourth of the six children. She had also acquired another son called Wazir, who had joined their household for general help, when his widowed mother couldn't afford to bring him up on her own. Wazir soon latched on to Bebeji as a mother, due to her kind and caring nature, and spent the rest of his life with his adopted family.

Sham was a proud man and stood by his principles, so sometimes would rub his bosses and work colleagues the wrong way. A few of his transfers were for professional development, others were due to his differences with his bosses. By the end of his fifth assignment, he had lost interest in his profession and saw little value in the job he was doing. Upon being offered a sixth posting to a remote, difficult to reach hilly area, he decided to give it a last chance. He sent his family back home to his village Lalheri until he was certain of his future. At the end of 1917, Basso at the age of 36, returned with her seven children to the family's ancestral home in Lalheri, to continue life in a mud house like the one where she had grown up. With their savings she was able to afford some basic comforts and household belongings.

A year later, after a disagreement with his English boss over a derogatory racist remark, Sham resigned from his job and joined the family in the ancestral village. He started teaching in a local high school at a significantly reduced salary. His income was supplemented by rent from their agricultural land. Basso worked hard to meet the needs of her family, trying to run the household in their financially deteriorating position.

A drop in job status and the guilt of seeing his family suffer due to financial problems led Sham to remorse, depression and drinking. Three years later, on May 3, 1921, Sham passed away after a short illness. Basso was widowed at the age of 39. The full responsibility of bringing up her seven young children, on a limited income from the family land, fell on her shoulders. The skills she had learned as a teenager from her mother to run a farming family home, proved to be useful. But the chores of a farmer's wife weren't the only skills required to run the farm. Her adopted son Wazir, who was in his teens, shared some of her load and took over many of the manual farming tasks. As was a custom at the time, Basso's mother Raj moved in with the family to help, just like Sham's maternal grandmother had moved in to look after him after he lost his mother. Fortunately, Basso's elder sister was also married in Lalheri to Jaimal Singh Sumal [who was not a direct relative, but was probably from the same ancestral branch as Kartar], which gave them much needed help and support. Later on, her brother Hazara and his family also moved to Lalheri village.

When Sham died, Basso's fifteen-year-old eldest daughter Karam Kaur had been married for a year. She was still living with them, in keeping with the custom of a child bride staying with her family until puberty, when a maclava [departure] ceremony took place. Karam moved in with her husband Hukam's family a year later when she was sixteen. A few months after that Hukam left for Kenya to join his elder brother Chanan who had settled in Kenya in 1920.

Sham's death was the start of dark days and struggles for Basso in the male dominated society of the 1920s, but she always prioritized her four sons' education. When times were difficult, she sold her jewelry to make ends meet. Apart from dowries for her two daughters, she just kept one gold necklace to marry her four sons with. She never sold any land even in difficult times because she saw it as her only source of income, and she believed it was her sons' inheritance.

In 1924, three years after their father's death, Kartar's 16-year-old elder brother Gurmukh left school without appearing for his ninth-class examination and went to Calcutta to look for a job as a car driver. His desperate attempt to supplement the family's income in a tough job market was unsuccessful and he returned to the village after a few months. A year later in 1925, when Karam's brother-in-law visited India, the family arranged for her to accompany him to Kenya to join her husband, Hukam. This is when Gurmukh decided to join them, to find employment in Kenya, and to support his family back home. He was seventeen at the time.

After his father's death Kartar was a lost soul trying to find a purpose in life. Apart from looking for adventures in life as teenagers do, he started taking an interest in religion. Without a father's guidance and with a mother fully occupied in bringing up a large family and managing the farm, Kartar looked for alternative ways of life. He ran away from home twice to join a camp of sadhus [holy men] and was becoming a handful for a single mother. This is when she decided to send him to Kenya to join his elder brother.

The money that the brothers were able to send from Africa helped to support the family back home. In 1937, this money helped to replace the original family mud walled house with a two-story brick house, to which an animal outhouse and fodder storage areas were added. In keeping with the tradition of having a baitak [living/reception room away from the house], the family built a large brick room in the entrance lane to the village.

KARTAR WITH HIS NIECES AND YOUNGER BROTHER GURDIAL ON THE STAIRCASE OF THE TWO-STORY BRICK HOUSE, LALHERI, INDIA, 1963.

THEIR FATHER'S NAME "SHAM SINGH SUMAL 1937" ENGRAVED ON THE MAIN GATE.

The family had earned the respect of the whole village. The brothers in their smart western suits and ties, their wives smartly dressed in salwaar-kameez suits made from imported material, and the children wearing clothes and shoes bought in Kenya inevitably incited the envy of some villagers.

The following incident shows how the family was perceived by others. During a visit to Lalheri, Kartar's five-month-old nephew Bali, developed high fever and diarrhea. When his condition deteriorated in the evening, Kartar hired a tanga, a horse drawn carriage, to take his sister and sick nephew to Ludhiana hospital. Wazir accompanied them. As soon as they had crossed over the Doraha canal bridge, robbers on horseback started following them. A well-dressed young couple in elegant, imported clothes, with a child and a domestic help to take care of their needs, riding in a mode of transportation only a few could afford, were a perfect target for robbers to loot. Wazir, with his heart set on farming, had little time or desire to take care of his appearance, so he was easily mistaken as a domestic help. Traveling late at night made the situation worse. Fortunately, it all turned out well when the tanga driver, a master of his trade, kept the robbers at bay by picking up speed over the dirt roads until they reached the town of Sahnewal five miles away. By then the sun was rising so the robbers gave up their chase, leaving them safe but shaken.

Unfortunately, there is no record of a family picture taken in 1942/43 which were the golden years of Bebeji's life. After overcoming 21 years of hard work and financial struggles by making good judgment calls in planning her children's path in life, she was finally able to enjoy a stress-free life, surrounded by a successful and thriving family. At the age of 60 all her wishes for her family had been fulfilled. It was time to enjoy the ultimate reward of being a beloved mother, mother-in-law and grandmother.

Little did she know how the political situation in the world would bring her happy little world tumbling down. The second world war, food shortages, unemployment, steep inflation, changes in immigration policies in Kenya and finally the partition of India would bring pain and suffering to her and her family. The struggles of the years 1943-1949 are well captured in the letters from Kartar's two brothers, Gurmukh and Shangara, who remained stuck in India due to circumstances beyond their control.

PART 2
Letters to a Brother
(1943 - 1949)

GURMUKH, AUTHOR
OF LETTERS

KARTAR, RECIPIENT
OF LETTERS

SHANGARA, AUTHOR
OF LETTERS

Introduction

In the spring of 1942, all of Kartar's siblings and their families were together in India. This joyful time of family togetherness came to an end in the summer of 1942, when his elder sister, Karam Kaur and her family returned to Kenya, at the end of their long leave.

The seats for Kartar and his family's return journey were booked on S.S. Tilawa sailing on November 20, 1942. His youngest son was unwell and his mother begged him to stay a little longer to spend time with her while all the brothers were together. Feeling tempted to extend his leave, Kartar went to see his friend Swaran Singh. Together, they planned to claim sick leave once again, and visited the BI [British India] office in Ludhiana to obtain sick leave certificates. They were relieved to learn that they could obtain these by paying a fee of 20 rupees, with no requirement for a medical examination. With the certificates in hand, they sent telegrams to the British India Shipping office in Bombay to cancel their ship reservations to Mombasa.

A few weeks later rumors started circulating about a Japanese attack on a ship carrying Indian passengers. Kartar soon received a letter from the shipping agent Mackinnon Mackenzie & Co. Ltd, to confirm that S.S. Tilawa had been attacked by the Japanese and a number of passengers were lost at sea. They also added that all shipping between Bombay and Mombasa was suspended indefinitely, until further notice. Destiny had played its hand by saving Kartar and his family's lives, but the news hit Kartar hard as a number of his friends lost their lives. His friend Pritam Singh from village Moga lost all of his family except one daughter, Tej. Another friend, Maggar Singh lost his wife, Harbhajan.

When shipping resumed in early 1943, only high priority passengers were issued tickets. Railway workers came under this category but not their families. Kartar was able to secure a place for himself on a ship sailing from Bombay on March 9, 1943, but had to leave his family behind.

The year 1942 brought changes to Kenya's immigration laws for Indians, which barred Kartar's brothers Gurmukh and Shangara from returning to Kenya. This second part of the book consists of translations of letters written between the years 1943 and 1949 by the two brothers to Kartar in Kenya. The letters capture the struggles of four families living on the meager income from their small family farm in India and the low salary of Kartar, the sole earner in Kenya. With this limited income, Gurmukh, as head of the family, faced the challenging task of balancing the daily needs of seventeen members of the joint family living under one roof, with the pressing need to buy more land to secure future needs. Each year brought fresh challenges and obstacles in the lives of the family.

Almost all letters depict the two brothers' deep desire to return to an economically better life in Kenya, while struggling with the practicalities of new rules and regulations for entry and the reduced chances of their employability. The frustrating challenges of shipping and obtaining work permits for Kenya, hindered their efforts to escape the hardships of their lives in India. Having lived in Kenya previously they knew what Kenya had to offer and couldn't see a better future for their families in India.

Impact of World Events on the Family in India

During the six-year period, 1943 to 1949, the following world events shaped and influenced the lives of Kartar's family in India.

Restrictions on immigration of Indians to Kenya

With the British government preoccupied by the Second World War, the Europeans in Kenya gained greater control of governing the country which led to revived demands for self-government and restrictions on Indian immigration. Europeans claimed that Indians were swamping the country and hindering the advancement of Africans. They challenged the loyalty of Indians to their adopted country of Kenya, citing the money they constantly sent to India from their earnings in East Africa. These letters provide a better understanding of the necessity to transfer money to families in India.

They wanted to stop Indian immigration while keeping it open for Europeans, as in South Africa. In 1942, this led to laws restricting Indian immigration to Kenya. It was ironic considering that two years earlier the Compulsory Service Bill was passed to restrict skilled Indian workers from leaving the country. The Service Bill was in anticipation of a looming war in Europe spreading to East Africa and the need for mechanics and drivers to support the war efforts.

The new immigration law allowed only Indians 'on leave' from their jobs in Kenya to re-enter the country. New Indian immigrants and those who had left the country after resigning from their jobs in Kenya, were subjected to the new restrictions. To keep the door open for Indian migrants for crucial jobs in Kenya, a new process was introduced. An offer of a job from an employer in Kenya had to be approved by the Kenyan authorities. A visa for Kenya was only issued in India on obtaining this permit in the form of a "Special Endorsement Certificate". During the high unemployment period of 1942-1947 amongst Indians in Kenya, these permits were very restricted and difficult to obtain, especially for those without any special technical skills. When the economies in Europe and Kenya stabilized after the war, these restrictions were somewhat relaxed.

Shipping between India and Kenya

The Japanese aggression in the Far East pulled Britain and its colonies into the war. Britain started using some of the passenger ships on the India-Kenya route for transportation of soldiers fighting in the Far East, mainly Burma. Starting in 1943, passenger shipping services between India and Kenya remained very restricted, unreliable, erratic and chaotic for the following three years. In desperation, some of the passengers resorted to traveling on the dangerous dhows sailing between India and Kenya.

Steep Inflation in India

During the years following 1943, India went through one of its highest rates of inflation. In 1943 the inflation rate was 54%. The 1943 famine in Bengal and the need to divert resources for war efforts were the two main causes of this high inflation. The suffering and struggles caused by the inflation is captured in these letters.

Communal Riots Following Partition of India into Two Countries (India and Pakistan)

Britain granted Independence to India on August 15, 1947, as a country divided into two, a Hindu India and a Muslim Pakistan. This divided two communities that had lived in integrated societies for centuries. The somewhat random line drawn by British bureaucrats to divide the country triggered riots, mass casualties, and a colossal wave of migration, with millions of Muslims heading towards Pakistan, Hindus and Sikhs heading towards India.

India's Independence and Gandhi's Death

During this six-year period the two major events for which India is remembered are India's independence in 1947 and Gandhi's death on January 30, 1948. What stands out in the letters is the absence of any mention of these two events. Was it because the international awareness of events of such magnitude did not necessitate a mention? Or was it because these events had little initial impact on everyday life in small villages of India?

CHAPTER 1

1943
Separation from Family

After a long break in India, Kartar left for Kenya on a ship sailing from Bombay on March 9, 1943. He left home with just sixteen rupees in his pocket. In Bombay he got an unexpected but pleasant surprise when he received his wages backdated to November 1942. The Kenyan Government had decided to backdate pay for employees stranded in India due to the suspension of shipping services. He sent most of the money home.

This was the first time Kartar had been separated from his wife and four young children, two of whom needed medical care. His eldest son, Balbir suffered from epilepsy and the youngest, Binni (Balwinder) from a chronic chest condition. Due to the lack of a school for girls in their village, his five-year-old daughter, Barhi Guddi was sent to stay with Kartar's sister in a village 30 miles away.

For Kartar there was a pressing need to financially support the family back home, with mounting daily expenses plus the need to buy more land to sustain the families in the long run.

Farm animals are frequently mentioned in these letters. They were the livelihood of farmers and their presence was crucial for farming in Punjab. Bulls and camels were essential for plowing and drawing water from wells, for irrigation. Water buffalos' milk was more commonly used than cows' milk, to provide healthy nutrition for farming families.

From Gurmukh Singh, 28.3.1943, Lalheri

Dear brother Kartar Singh, Sat Siri Akal

I received your letter posted from Bombay and a telegram from Kenya on your safe arrival. We were all worried about your safety and feel so happy and relieved today.

On his way home, Amar Nath stopped here briefly and gave us the money, presents and letters that you sent with him from Bombay. I have given the gifts to Angrez Kaur.

From the Rs 400 you sent, after some other expenses and loan repayments, Rs 70 were deposited in the bank, and the remaining Rs 50 are to be used for our household expenses, which are no less than Rs 30 per month. Now I have a total of Rs 520 in the bank.

Do not worry about Balbir Singh's [Kartar's eldest son] illness. He is much better now and has only mild epileptic fits every 8-10 days. We saw a very capable doctor, who thinks Balbir will grow out of his fits as he gets older. He recommended a patent medicine, Peacock's Bromides, to be given to him daily for a week, followed by a short break. It is not easily available but I will look out for it. Barhi Guddi [Kartar's daughter] went to Ramgarh 10-15 days ago, and is studying there. Tomorrow, I will pick her up from Ramgarh and will take her to the doctor in Ludhiana for her eye medicine and will also buy Balbir Singh's medicine. I will keep you informed of how it helps him. Now, slowly Chani [Kartar's second son] is settling down without you. Binni's [Kartar's third son] health is better too, although he coughs sometimes. Waheguru [God] is the one who has granted life to our children and nothing is in our control. I will treat your children the same as all other children here and will look after them even better than my own. If I buy anything I will share it equally amongst them all, without being partial to my children.

I will keep working on acquiring more land. These days land is in great demand. We do not need to make a hasty decision. If I can arrange a daily paid worker at the farm, then I will have time to look for more land. Our whole family's expenses can't be covered by the income from our land.

I don't know why Shangara Singh has not written to me since you left. I will send him another letter today. Shangara Singh's address is:

Wireless Monitoring Office,
Counter Propaganda Directorate,
Bantony, Simla.

Balbir Singh has written this message for you "Sat Siri Akal, Balbir Singh". I held his hand to help him to write Sat Siri Akal [Sikh greetings], but he wrote his name himself. Chani was standing near me just now but seems to have run off somewhere. Don't worry about them.

Your loving brother, Gurmukh Singh

Kartar's two sisters Karam Kaur and Kartar Kaur were married to two Mangat brothers from Ramgarh, a village frequently mentioned in the letters. The elder sister lived in Kenya and the younger sister lived in the Mangat family home in Ramgarh, India. The following letter was written after the death of their father-in-law, Master Inder Singh. The Indian tradition of funeral costs being partially borne by the families of daughters-in-law created an extra burden on the already stretched family finances.

From Gurmukh Singh, 21.4.1943, Lalheri

Dear brother Kartar Singh, Sat Siri Akal.

I received your letter dated 30th March and got all your news. Hopefully you have found accommodation by now. Balbir, Guddi, Chani & Binni are all well and happily settled here. Don't worry about them at all. I bought Guddi's eye medicine and a bottle of Peacock's Bromides for Rs 8, from Ludhiana and Balbir Singh is a lot better with this medicine.

You must have heard the news from Ramgarh. On 13th April, Master Inder Singh passed away suddenly after a short illness. This is really sad as he was a big support to everyone at Ramgarh.

They are finalizing plans for hungama [a traditional ceremony after someone's death]. We might be expected to give clothes and jewelry to the family. Our expenses will be Rs 250-300, as the cost of gold is over Rs 85 now. If we include gold rings for the two brothers-in-law, it will cost us another Rs 125, bringing the total to Rs 500, which will leave me with nothing as that is all I have left. We will do what is expected of us. This is another unexpected expense that has risen.

Shangara Singh came for 3-4 days during his holidays, and returned to Simla yesterday with Jaswant Kaur [Shangara's wife] and the boys.

Sat Siri Akal from all of us, the children and Bebeji.

Your loving brother, Gurmukh Singh

From Gurmukh Singh, 8.5.1943, Lalheri

Dear brother Kartar Singh, Sat Siri Akal.

I received your letter and a postcard, but please don't send a card in future as it can be read by others before reaching me.

Do not worry about the impact of war and carry on working with a peaceful mind.

Yesterday I was able to purchase 23.5 bighas [15 acres] of land for Rs 1250. I have paid a Rs 200 deposit and the balance needs to be paid within 15 days. I will arrange to get this money together by borrowing from our relatives or somewhere else. I can also use the family jewelry to borrow cash. I had Rs 500 in total, which leaves me with Rs 300, after paying the deposit. Out of this, we might be required to pay Rs 200 for the old man's hungama in Ramgarh.

Don't worry about the kids. Waheguru will protect them. You and I will continue to take care of them. Hopefully these times will pass well.

Love from Bebeji, Gurbachan Kaur [Gurmukh's wife] and me, Sat Siri Akal from the rest.

From Gurmukh Singh, 2.6.1943, Lalheri

Dear brother Kartar Singh, Sat Siri Akal

The total cost for the land was Rs 1275. I borrowed Rs 200 from Atma Ram Mistry, and took a loan from Khanna for the remaining sum. I will pay back the money when I receive it from you.

I sorted out Ramgarh's hungama from the Rs 95 that you sent. We spent Rs 65 on clothes and bought 3 kameezes [shirts], 1 ghagra [long skirt], and gave some of the clothes from home worth at least Rs 75, so altogether the clothes were worth Rs 150. They did not accept any jewelry or money.

Eight families in our village have a claim on 25 bighas [16 acres] of the village common land. All families have paid their share of Rs 70 each, to register a case. It will be well worth it, to acquire 3.5 bigha [2 acres] land, worth at least Rs 400, by spending Rs 70 on the case.

We will definitely need to buy a camel in 5-10 days' time, which will cost us no less than Rs 300, as bullocks and camels are very expensive these days.

On 31st May, I met Bachan Singh of Pingowal, at Ludhiana station. He had just arrived from Kenya. I enquired about your well-being, but he said he had set off from Africa soon after you reached there. He sailed from Mombasa in a dhow on 12th April and arrived in Bombay on 24th May, finally reaching Ludhiana 7 days later on the 31st. What he told me about his perilous journey on a dhow was really distressing. The dhow he traveled on was meant for 40 people but was overloaded with 120 passengers, two of whom died on the way. Once or twice their lives were saved with great difficulty in the storms. They had left from Mombasa with two months rations, which were all used up in just 1 month and 12 days. He said he had learned a lesson the hard way and will never ever travel in a dhow under any circumstances. That day the poor fellow was very shaken up.

I got Shangara Singh's letter yesterday and all is well with him. With his children over there, he is finding it financially difficult to support his family.

Sat Siri Akal from all of us.

As always, your loving brother Gurmukh Singh, Lal-heri.

From Gurmukh Singh, 27.6.1943, Lalheri

Dear brother Kartar Singh ji, Sat Siri Akal

You wrote about not sending you the list of expenses, but that will never happen. I will definitely keep sending an account of the money spent, to both you and Shangara Singh. One reason is that if I was in your shoes then our expenses would seem too high to me, without knowing where the money is being spent. Secondly if I am not accountable to anyone and do not give you a breakdown of expenses then there is a danger of me being tempted to waste it on unnecessary things. Giving an account of my expenses helps me to control my spending. I would be grateful if you obtain a notebook and start copying all the expenses in it.

Accounts from the day you left until today and the balance left over. Note all amounts in Rs-Ana-Paisa							
INCOME				EXPENSES			
The cash I had on the day you left	45	0	0	Household expenses 15 Mar 43 to 15 Apr 43	61	11	0
Recieved Your money order from Bombay	400	0	0	Household expenses 16 Apr 43 to 2 Jun 43	199	0	0
Approximate amount from the sale of jaggery from the day you left	90	0	0	Money for the "Hakam" Land 3 ½ bigha (paid on 15 May 43)	56	0	0
Sent via Amar Nath	90	0		Expense for bakshi's land. Total approximate cost Rs1400	275	0	0
Withdrawn from my account	400	0		Atma Ram handyman (return of money borrowed to buy the land)	200	0	0
Exchanged big cattle for a cow	44	0	0	Loaned money to two new sanjhis	200	0	0
Check you sent	661	4	0	Household expenses 2 Jun 43 to 26Jun 43	108	0	0
				Bought Camel	300	0	0
				Given to Angrez kaur	11	4	0
Total	1730	4	0	Total	2410	15	0

Expence	2410	15	0
Income	1730	4	0
Over spent	680	11	0

From 17 July 43 to 1 Sept 43			
Return fare Khanna to Ludhiana	0	14	0
Meal in Ludhiana	4	6	0
Mangoes 2 seers (3.5 lbs)	0	5	0
Biscuits ¼ seer	0	7	0
Shoes for Sarmukh Singh	1	8	0
Tea	0	4	0
Interest on loan from Khanna	5	0	0
Soap 1 seer (1.75 lbs)	0	12	0
Salwar Gurbachan Kaur 4 yards	4	0	0
Dyeing a turban	0	2	0
Repair of pocket watch	2	0	0
Umbrella repair	0	3	0
Expenses at Gurbachan Kaur's sister's wedding	11	8	0
Stiching of 2 shirts for Gurmukh Singh	10	15	0
Dyeing of Chunni (head scarf)	0	2	0
Lemon	0	2	0
Fares for travel to Khanna-Ramgarh -Ludihana-Jandali and back	2	0	0
Kameez for Bebeji	1	8	0
Washing powder 4 seer	1	4	0
Soap 1 seer	0	12	0
Oil grinder repair	1	0	0
Donation to a transgender (Khanna)	1	0	0
Aerogram letter	1	0	0
Meat 3 ½ seer	1	0	0

EXAMPLE OF EXPENSE SHEETS KEPT BY GURMUKH. NOTE: 1 RUPEE PAYMENT TO A TRANSGENDER, AN INDIAN TRADITION FOR GOOD HEALTH OF A CHILD. WAS THIS FOR BALBIR'S HEALTH?

Balbir Singh started attending school on 2nd June, but a day or two later he started having fits which lasted for 4 to 5 days. My main concern is that Waheguru [God] keeps him healthy. This worries me all the time and I pray to Waheguru to enable me to return your amanat [your precious child] that you left in my care, in good health. Now for the past 20 days he has been absolutely fine and is attending school, so there is nothing to worry about. Binni's health is also better than before now. Chani is hale and hearty, and is not too sad, although he misses you very much.

Regarding renewing Angrez Kaur's [Kartar's wife] passport, I will need two to three months' notice after you have finalized your family's travel date. Nowadays railway service is included in active service so hopefully, you will get assistance in getting shipping reservations and passports renewed. Also get the special endorsement certified to get an entry permit stamped on the passport.

Love from all the children and Sat Siri Akal from the rest of us.

Your brother Gurmukh Singh

From Gurmukh Singh, 18.7.1943, Lalheri

Dear brother Kartar Singh, Sat Siri Akal.

I will keep a lookout and will inform you about any land that becomes available for us to buy. The sad state of affairs is that there is no land available for tilling. It is only available as security for lending money. You cannot rely on this land as the borrower can easily redeem it at any time. Money spent on land is like a safe deposit.

We now have four bullocks and a camel, for farming. We have planted sugarcane on 4 bighas, cotton on 10 bighas and 17 bighas have been allocated for maize. The land is on a 'nine shares' basis (7 shares for us, 2 shares for the two helpers on the farm).

Amar Singh [Angrez's brother] got a tabeez [sacred necklace] made in Badochi, for Balbir Singh to wear, but after being healthy for 10 to 12 days, the problem started again. Damodhwallah Sant [holy person] gave us some medicine and a tabeez along with it. The Guru has been merciful since then and for a month now, Balbir Singh has not had any problem at all, not even a minor one.

Binni's health is much better than before. He can stand now and walks with support. He has not had any fever, but always has a little cough and a rattly chest.

You wrote that you have got a promotion at work. This is very good news. To be honest this is good fortune for all of us and is a merit earned for our good deeds. I pray that God gives you even more strength so that you can better yourself further. Your improvement benefits all of us. Do not worry at all about the children.

Your brother Gurmukh Singh

From Shangara Singh, 17.8.1943, Simla

Brother Kartar Singh Ji, Sat Siri Akal.

I received your letter yesterday via Gurmukh Singh. The reason for not writing to you earlier was to save postage money as I knew he had already given you all the news. He forwards all your letters to me so I get all your news. I was sad that I could not meet you before your departure.

You must already know of the situation here. I brought Jaswant Kaur [his wife] here about 2-3 months ago as there was difficulty regarding cooking. I could have managed to cook for myself if it had been a matter of a day or two, but now with everyone here, it is proving difficult to make ends meet, let alone sending anything home. Everything is very expensive and the pay is very low. Prices are increasing on a daily basis. Whatever I earn gets spent straight away. I have found someone to start sharing the rent with me. Then I will send the children back home.

I am enclosing some photos with this letter. Give Nanhi and Lakha's [Shangara's two sons] photos to Bibiji Karam Kaur [Kartar's elder sister in Kenya] and remind her that this is the same Nanhi who pooped on her clothes and soiled them. He is very mischievous. I guess some of his poop stains are still on Bibiji's clothes! Lakha has grown a lot, even more than Nanhi. He has started to talk much more than Nanhi. He runs about a lot and is healthier than Nanhi.

One advantage of my job is that I get to know the situation around the world and also about Kenya. Do you intend to buy a lottery ticket this time? I will get to know the results anyway, which are expected to be announced at 11 o'clock on 22nd August.

I do get to find out a little bit of the employment situation in Kenya, through my work, but continue checking with your acquaintances too and keep me informed of any opportunities and the wages in Africa, as a mechanic or with the Power and Lighting company. I heard that there is a great demand by the government for electricians and their wages are also very good. On receiving my letter, please post the enclosed sheet of paper to 'Cable and Wireless, PO Box 77, Nairobi'. If they reply to this, forward their reply to me as they regularly request further certificates and applications.

Sat Siri Akal to all of you.

Your brother Shangara Singh.

From Shangara Singh, 2.12.43, Simla

Brother Kartar Singh Ji, Sat Siri Akal. We are all well over here and pray to Waheguru for your wellbeing.

I went home for 15 days at Diwali. We all missed you a lot.

Balbir Singh has been well for a long time, and has had no fits since we got the tabeez. While I was there,

Balbir Singh kept asking me daily "Chachaji [Uncle], when are we going to Africa?" He is really keen to come to you. He has made progress in his studies too. He still attends Hari Om School. Do not worry about anything. Binni's health is better than before. Barhi Guddi had also come from Ramgarh before my arrival. Bebeji is fine but she coughs every now and then as the weather is getting colder now. We received your photo and the children were very happy to see it. Balbir Singh keeps it with him all the time.

We have heard that all ships are fully booked and no seats are available so I will continue working over here until I am able to come to Africa.

Please reply to my letter soon, otherwise I start worrying about you. Sat Siri Akal to you and everyone else.

Your brother, Shangara Singh

From Gurmukh Singh, 11.12.43, Lalheri

Dear brother Kartar Singh, Sat Siri Akal

We are hearing from everyone that due to the war, traveling by ship is very chaotic and difficult these days and you can't get any seats. On 1st December, I sent all our passports to the District Commissioner by registered mail. Nowadays renewal takes as long as a new passport, but hopefully they will be ready by early March.

Shangara Singh has no plans to continue with his present job as he can barely support himself on his low wages. The staff members at his work asked for a "high cost of living" allowance but the office management refused it.

Things are very unsettled at present and we don't know how long this uncertainty will last. It is difficult to source even necessities these days and everything is very expensive. Everyday household items like salt are in short supply and are being rationed. One has to go to town daily to source basic necessities. I believe the situation in Africa must be the same. Nowadays even with money in their pockets, people are dying of hunger due to scarcity of food. Even with Rs 100 in your pocket, you can wander all around Khanna bazaar without being able to buy anything.

Regarding food and milk, you will understand that it is difficult to make sure everyone gets a portion of milk as the whole household has to make do with the limited supply from just one buffalo.

Sat Siri akal from all of us, Balbir Singh and all kids. Love from Bebeji.

Your loving brother, Gurmukh Singh

CHAPTER 2

1944
Shipping Hurdles

The letters of 1944 highlight the shipping problems and difficulties in securing tickets due to passenger ships being used for world war efforts in the Far East. The limited, unpredictable and chaotic shipping between India and Kenya resulted in thousands of families being stranded in India. Some desperate men with no income, resorted to traveling on overloaded, unsafe and flimsy dhows. People who were already stretched for cash, often had to wait in Bombay for weeks, even months, on the off chance of getting a passage at short notice.

Recollections of the 'joint family life' during her
stay in India (1942-1945)
by Kartar's daughter, Perminder (Barhi Guddi)

I was five when we arrived in India so my recollections of our stay are quite vague. Most little girls in those days were referred to as Guddi so everyone called me Barhi [elder] Guddi and my cousin sister Jasminder was called Choti [younger] Guddi.

When we boarded the ship at Mombasa in June 1942, we were full of excitement at the prospect of spending four months with the extended family in our homeland. Mama and us four kids had third class tickets so we stayed on the deck of the ship. My dad (Kartar Singh) being a railway employee, was allocated a second-class cabin, so he used to take us up to his room to give us a bath. I had never seen a bathtub before so I started screaming and clung to him in fear when he lowered me into the bath water, which felt like an extension of the sea. I was terrified that I would slip down into the sea and drown. I dreaded having a bath throughout the ten-day long journey.

Our four months stay got extended due to the Second World War and difficulties to get passage for families. My dad left in March 1943, to resume duty in Kenya. Uncle Gurmukh Singh took responsibility to look after us and to ensure that we attended schools. My elder brother Balbir Singh started attending a local school in Lalheri, but there were no schools for girls in our village. So, my aunt Kartar Kaur kindly offered to take me to Ramgarh. My school in Ramgarh consisted of two rooms in a local Gurudwara [temple], with classes up to year five. A middle-aged couple taught us.

My aunt looked after me well, but I sorely missed my family. I remember feeling very homesick and longing for my Mama's love and warmth. Even little reprimands used to make me feel very sad. In addition to my two cousins, there were two other second cousins living in the family home with their widowed mother. They had recently lost their father to Blackwater fever in East Africa. So, five of us needed to have our long hair combed in the mornings. Being the youngest and far away from my family, I always felt very shy and timid. I would stand meekly in a corner, waiting for my turn. Sometimes, my cousins' grandma Atto felt sorry for me and offered to do my hair, but she was quite rough with my tangles. It used to hurt but I never complained.

I looked forward to my school holidays when one of my uncles would come to pick me up. We had to walk two miles to Sahnewal station to catch the train. The hot, burning sand used to get into my open sandals in the summer heat, making it very difficult to walk. The journey ended in a two mile long walk from Khanna station at the other end, but the joy of being with my Mama and three brothers made it all worthwhile. We could see Khanna railway station and the trains from the rooftop of our Lalheri house. Trains were the main mode of travel in those days.

My grandma [Bebeji] always accompanied me to the outskirts of the village whenever I left for Ramgarh after my holidays. She felt very sad once, when she was unable to do so, as she had to accompany my aunt [Jaswant Kaur] to the fields. Luckily for her, we missed our train and had to return home. She was overjoyed to get another chance to see her beloved granddaughter off properly. She doted on her grandchildren, and always said she detested trains as they took her family away from her.

Bebeji was short, fair complexioned and soft spoken. She had deep set eyes. She was left-handed and used to drape her chuni [head scarf] the wrong way round, from left to right. I never saw her quarreling with anyone. I have fond memories of my gentle, caring and affectionate grandmother, who fussed over us, especially after my dad had gone to Kenya. Mama had a close relationship with her and they both looked after each other.

Our ancestral home in Lalheri consisted of a large, airy and bright main room with several windows and two doors. This room led to two small, dark windowless inner store-rooms. As a child I was petrified of going on my own into these two eerie looking rooms. There was a cupboard in the main room where jaggery [concentrated product of cane sugar] was stored. A family photo taken during our previous visit in 1937, hung on the wall opposite this cupboard. When no-one was around, I could not resist the temptation to eat a piece or two of sweet jaggery. I always tried to hide it from the watchful eyes of the grownups in the picture because I believed that they could see me. Our house was the only one in the village with a big bathroom *and a tap with running water. I remember the neighborhood ladies visiting to have a bath or to wash their clothes.*

At Diwali, my dad's cousin brother used to make mithai [Indian sweets] in our courtyard. That was the only time of the year we had mithai. Meat curry [probably mutton], another rarity, was cooked for the evening meal. We used to light diyas [little earthen pots containing a cotton wick and rapeseed oil] but there were no fireworks.

As a child I was not aware of the struggles my Mama was going through at the time. My baby brother Binni was recovering from pneumonia and my elder brother Balbir Singh was going through a rough patch with his epilepsy. Under dire economic conditions, high unemployment, no job prospects, rationing, steep inflation, erratic shipping, life got very tough for the grownups stuck in the homeland, but us children were oblivious to all these problems.

From Gurmukh Singh, 5.1.1944, Lalheri

Dear brother Kartar Singh Ji, Sat Siri Akal

I met Pritam Singh Ji [a family friend] at Ramgarh and told him that Kartar Singh is arranging tickets for his family. He said Mackinnon Mackenzie are not doing much to help with passages, not even for families of Railways or Government staff, and waiting in Bombay for a passage can be very expensive and problematic. Find out how other families are obtaining their tickets. Pritam Singh is trying to arrange tickets through his contacts with Mackinnon Mackenzie in Bombay, by paying Rs 151 [sweetener], instead of Rs 101 per ticket for the deck. Nowadays everyone is trying hard to get tickets by doing so. This is still a lot cheaper than flying, which some of our friends are resorting to, but that is beyond our means.

We will certainly try to send Angrez Kaur and the kids with Pritam Singh.

If you are able to arrange their tickets through Mackinnon Mackenzie, then try to obtain 1 or 2 extra tickets at the same time, so either Shangara Singh or I can accompany them. At Rs 151 per ticket, it will cost one person at least Rs 200 to travel up to Mombasa, that is if the ship sails within 4-5 days. If we have to wait for a month in Bombay, then the expense will be beyond our means. Whoever leaves will be fine, but the ones left behind will have more problems. Men can think rationally and get along in all situations, but women can't. They quarrel over minor things.

Vaccination certificates for Angrez Kaur & the kids are with me. I think they are valid for three years. The 'customs form' from Mombasa is in my safekeeping. I have sent all our passports for renewal. They have been forwarded after completion of all official formalities at Police Station and Administrative Offices. Hopefully they will be done and returned during the month of January. All ready to go after that. Let me know if I need to make any other arrangements.

Shangara Singh is here on ten days leave. There is some uncertainty about the future of his department, Wireless Monitoring Office, Counter Propaganda Directorate due to leakage of information from the department, so he has decided to resign from that job. He is hoping to get a job elsewhere, perhaps in Jagadhri, if the wages offered are good.

Your brother Gurmukh Singh

PS- Balbir Singh is sitting next to me now and has asked me to write "Sat Siri Akal to Chachaji [Kartar]"

The following letter portrays how Indian women who had lived independently in Kenya found it difficult to settle back in India in a joint family environment. They longed for the independence they had enjoyed in making decisions in Kenya. That attraction outweighed the joy of living near their loved ones in the country of their birth and childhood

From Gurmukh, dated 6.2.1944, Lalheri

Dear brother Kartar Singh, Sat Siri Akal.

Your letter dated 10.1.1944 arrived here on 25th January, 1944. The letter you wrote to Angrez Kaur, has been given to her. I was very saddened to read about the burn on your hand.

I have not yet received a reply from Mackinnon Mackenzie regarding Angrez Kaur and the kids' passage. Pritam Singh of Ramgarh told me that Mackinnon Mackenzie can only guarantee passage for Railway workers but not their wives or children. He is going to Bombay to arrange tickets through his cousin, who is a secretary at the Seamen's Association. I asked him to try for us too but he already has a long list of people wanting tickets. He seemed reluctant about Angrez Kaur and the kids accompanying him, so I told him that one of us will be with them until they board the ship at Bombay and Kartar Singh will meet them in Mombasa. It will be very difficult for Angrez Kaur to wait for a month in Bombay on her own. You know how expensive it is to stay in Bombay.

Today I have sent letters by registered post to the Under Secretary, Punjab Govt, Lahore and to DC Ludhiana, so hopefully the passports will arrive soon, and we can get them endorsed in April [visa for Kenya]. At present I am more worried about what would be best for Angrez Kaur and the kids. Thinking back, it might have been easier to obtain their tickets as accompanying dependents if they had traveled with you, but then that would have probably caused a delay in your departure.

I hope you won't get offended by what I have written below.

Women who have lived independently in Africa, find it very difficult to live in a joint family in India, whether it is your wife or mine. My wife has to stay here out of compulsion as I am stuck here, but your wife has the option to go to you and that is what she wants. You know that Angrez Kaur can't have the same life that she had in Africa so she feels the need to get there as soon as possible, for a better and peaceful life. My wife would want the same if she was in her place.

I will try to send her to you as soon as possible. She understandably feels upset that her kids are suffering, because they are used to a better life in Africa.

They are used to a life where they always had good nourishment with no shortage of milk. It is difficult to give them those facilities and that standard of living over here. Their treatment from others is beyond my control, but I will make sure that they are not treated any worse than other kids. In a big family, I can't give her preferential treatment, but if she needs anything I will get it for her.

Shangara Singh has left the job at Simla as it was too expensive to live there. You have written that one of us should come over. My opinion is that you should try to arrange tickets for Angrez Kaur and the kids. Sending Shangara Singh and Jaswant Kaur (& kids) with Angrez Kaur will cost a lot but he will probably be able to arrange employment quicker than I would.

Your loving brother, Gurmukh Singh

From Gurmukh Singh, 2.3.1944, Lalheri

Dear brother Kartar Singh Ji, may you have a long life, Sat Siri Akal.

Angrez Kaur and the kids' renewed passport has arrived and has now been sent for special endorsement. I gave April as their intended travel date, and received a reply yesterday from the Under Secretary, Lahore stating that they will return the passport at the end of March. Angrez Kaur will now hopefully come on the same ship as Pritam Singh, if her passage gets sorted in time. The arrangements that you have made over there have little value here because nobody gives any credence to them. Even people whose tickets had been confirmed a long time ago, have been informed by Mackinnon Mackenzie that their passage may be canceled without further notice. I have not received any reply from the shipping agents.

I always keep you in mind but you must wait patiently, we will try to hasten things. If their passage gets arranged at short notice even then I will not delay them due to lack of rupees. I will somehow arrange to borrow rupees from someone but if I can't, then I will wire you.

I gave Rs 200 to Angrez Kaur on the day I received your money, so that she can slowly start the preparations. The things you asked for will be sent with her. The children with Waheguru's mercy are all hale and hearty. Binni is much healthier than before. The wartime difficulties are increasing on a daily basis. I do not know what will happen in the future.

Sat Siri Akal from all of us, love from Bebeji.

Your brother Gurmukh Singh, Post Office Khanna.

SPECIAL ENDORSEMENT ON ANGREZ KAUR SUMAL'S PASSPORT TO
ENTER KENYA, ISSUED BY "POLITICAL DEPARTMENT" IN LAHORE.
VALID FOR ONLY 30 DAYS. A RENEWAL WAS ISSUED IN BOMBAY.

From Gurmukh Singh, dated 26.3.1944, Lalheri

Dear brother Kartar Singh, Sat Siri Akal.

There is no reply from Bombay to date and we might
not receive it before Pritam Singh departs. He will
probably leave in mid-May. On our side, we will remain fully prepared for kids to go. As soon as I receive the endorsed passport, I will send it with the
vaccination certificates to Mackinnon Mackenzie in
Bombay. You should also write to Bombay to ask

them to book your family's passage with Pritam Singh although I have heard that they rarely pay attention to such requests.

Let me know about their meals too, whether to include these with the ship fare or send them with their own rations/grocery. Your stuff is ready- 2 trousers, 4 shirts, 2 underwear, 2 dhotis (wrap around cloth), 4 pairs of socks, 1 suit, 1 khaddar (cotton) suit. I will get clothes stitched for the kids, according to Angrez Kaur's wishes.

Aziz Balbir Singh has passed his exams and is in Class 3 now. He has had no fits at all. Binni is also running around now. Barhi Guddi is well and happily settled in Ramgarh, and is in class 1. Chani misses you a lot all the time.

There is a lot of unrest in Hindustan [India] and no-one knows when things might take a turn for the worse, in this "inquilab ka zamana" [revolutionary times, fight for India's independence]. Now is the time to live with each other in harmony and tolerance. Any disturbances will cost lives.

Your brother Gurmukh Singh

From Gurmukh Singh, dated 7.5.1944, Lalheri

Dear brother Kartar Singh Sat Siri Akal.

We received your letter and money order of Rs 397.

After receiving your wire [telegram sent to the shipping agents] Mackinnon Mackenzie wrote to me, from Bombay. A copy of their letter and my reply to them is enclosed. Everything is ready from our side, to leave whenever Pritam Singh informs us. If we are unable to arrange their passage with Pritam Singh, then I myself will see them off onto the ship at Bombay.

You have written that 'anyone who has lived in Kenya for 5 years is entitled to entry back from living abroad', but no such thing is mentioned in the copy of the cutting you sent. Passports for all of us have now been received. Along with the passport it is essential to have a Kenya entry permit. Angrez Kaur's passport had been endorsed for April so it has now been sent away for endorsement [visa] for May. The day I receive it, I will send it to Mackinnon Mackenzie along with vaccination certificates. There will be no delay on our part, rest is what Waheguru [God] wishes. He will ensure that they reach there safely. My focus is on this matter all the time. We are ready as of today and just waiting, although they may not depart from Bombay for another month. Angrez Kaur and children's clothes have all been stitched. Bibi Kartar Kaur [Kartar's sister] is also here, waiting to bid them farewell.

Your brother Gurmukh Singh.

Below are letters exchanged with Mackinnon
Mackenzie (MM):

From MM to Gurmukh Singh, dated 27.4.1944

Dear Sir,

**With reference to your letters of the 13th January,
we have to advise you that we have received the
following telegram from the Railway administra-
tion dated 26.4.44:**

**"Arrange passage Mrs Kartar Singh Sumal with
four children in the same boat as Pritam Singh's
departure."**

**Due to shortage of accommodation, we regret that
we cannot guarantee passage for Mrs Kartar Singh
Sumal and four children by the same departure by
which Mr. Pritam Singh travels. Should accommodation become available we will intimate to you the
date on which she should present herself and children to this office for traveling. In this connection
you should be in touch with Mr Pritam Singh. We
do not know when he will be in a fit condition. In
the meantime, you should be in possession of valid
passports and vaccination certificates for the above
lady and children.**

**We shall be glad to know whether Mrs. Kartar Singh
Sumal and children will be in a position to travel
alone, if we fail to secure passage for them by the
same departure by which Mr. Pritam Singh travels**

Please acknowledge receipt by return.

Yours faithfully,
MM & Co

Extract of letter from MM to Pritam Singh dated
28.4.1944

While your date of departure is coming nearer, we are receiving more telegraphic instructions to arrange family passages by the same departure by which you will be traveling. In this circumstance we are afraid whether we will be able to secure passage for your family.

However, we will write to you in due course whether you should report alone or with your family.

MM & Co. Bombay

Extract of letter from Pritam Singh to MM
4.5.1944

It is not acceptable to only give me a place as there are ladies and children who need to travel with me. My children should also definitely be given a place.

From Gurmukh Singh to MM 19.5.1944

Dear Sir,

Reference your letter K.U.R/R/2872 dated 27/4/44

I wish to inform you that I have been to see Mr. Pritam Singh, who has informed me to be ready and to wait for the telegram from you.

I humbly request you again to please try your utmost to arrange for the passage of Mrs Angrez Kaur along with Mr. Pritam Singh and if possible, send a separate telegram to my home address, advising the date of departure and the necessary charges can be paid on arrival there.

Enclosed please find passport No. A 25258 of Mrs Angrez Kaur and children, duly renewed and endorsed, along with five vaccination certificates [for Angrez Kaur and her four children] for your personal examination.

Please acknowledge receipt and oblige.

Yours
Gurmukh Singh

Telegram from Gurmukh Singh to MM 21.5.1944

Reference your K.U.R/R/2872 dated twenty seventh April, shall Angrez Kaur report with Pritam Singh twenty seventh instant reply.

From MM to Gurmukh Singh 22.5.1944

Mr. Gurmukh Singh Sumal,
C/O LalooRam, Ram Swaroop,
Khanna
K.U.R/R/5291
Bombay 22nd May

Dear Sir,

With reference to your letter of 19th May, 1944 and your telegram of 21st May regarding passage for Mrs Kartar Singh Sumal and four children, we have to advise that their names are on our waiting list. As soon as accommodation becomes available, we will advise you of the date on which they will be required to report here in order to travel.

We have on our waiting list a large number of applications for family passages. Owing to Government requirements, it is very difficult to obtain accommodation for civilians, and we cannot state whether we will be able to secure passage for them by the same departure by which Mr. Pritam Singh travels. According to present indications we are afraid we will not be in a position to arrange their passage in the near future, but we can assure you that every endeavor will be made to secure passage for them. We should also add that we have been advised by the agents B.I.S.N Co Ltd, Bombay that deck accommodation will not be available for civilians for some time. In this connection we confirm our telegram of even date reading as follows:

"Accommodation not available writing" The passport NO. A.25258 and the five vaccination certificates received with your letter under reply have been retained in this office.

Please acknowledge receipt and let us know whether Mrs. Sumal and children are prepared to travel alone when accommodation becomes available.

Yours faithfully,
M.M.& Co

Telegram from MM to Pritam Singh 27.5.1944

Bombay: Pritam Singh, Ramgarh, Sahnewal

Women with infants not allowed. Report here alone.

Bombay

Telegram from Pritam Singh to MM on same day

Not prepared to travel alone will wait for further sailing.

Pritam Singh.

From Gurmukh Singh to MM, 27.5.1944

Mackinnon Mackenzie & Co
Ballard Road
Bombay

Dear Sir,

I beg to acknowledge the receipt of your letter K.U.R/R/5291 dated 22/5/44

As stated in your letter, Angrez Kaur is prepared to travel alone, with other civilian passengers, than to wait for an indefinite period. Almost six months have already passed since her name went on the waiting list and after such a long period there seems to be no hope in the near future, just discouraging replies.

As regards the question of civilian passengers mentioned in your letter I do agree with the hardships of the present time, but at the same time I like to have this point cleared, which I am afraid might cause annoyance that, a railway employee serving in the far away colony under conscription laws [law prohibiting Indians in special jobs from leaving the country] with no hope of leaving the services is in no way less than a military man. The simple word civilian does not suit this party and children, a person serving the same British Government Railway five thousand miles from his mother country with every risk for himself and his children as well who have to travel alone to reach to him in such risky times.

Lastly, keeping in view the parental love and anxiety of young children to reach their father. I hope and request earnestly that you will not delay longer the arrangements for their journey, if possible, with Mr Pritam Singh or alone at your earliest possibility

Yours faithfully
G. Singh Sumal

From Gurmukh Singh, 7.7.1944, Lalheri

Dear brother Kartar Singh Sat Siri Akal.

Pritam Singh received a wire around 18th June, telling him to come to Bombay on his own. He must have arrived in Kenya and explained everything to you, that I have tried very hard and left no stone unturned. I am trying my best.

I feel the right thing to do now is to wait here for their wire to instruct us to go to Bombay, otherwise who knows how long they will make us wait in Bombay. Also, if they themselves call us, then they will not refuse passage once we get there. I will try to arrange tickets at cost price, and will only pay extra, as a last resort.

I think you should send a telegram to Mackinnon Mackenzie saying:

"I am a government employee and I worry a lot about difficulties facing my family to obtain the tickets. Now my family is traveling on their own and hope they will not have any problems in Bombay."

Maybe after getting that letter, they won't demand extra money from us. I will be with them but don't mention this to them. Even in Bombay I will keep away from them, because if they see me, they will create more obstacles.

We have bought 3 bighas of farmland "Veryama wali zameen" for Rs 350 and also six and a half bighas of land from mussalman for Rs 260.

Land is difficult to get hold of nowadays but if any becomes available, we will buy it.

The children are all well. Sat Siri Akal from all of us.

Your loving brother, Gurmukh Singh

From Balbir Singh, 17.7.1944, Lalheri
(To his father Kartar Singh, who was in Nairobi)

Janab Chachaji Ji Sahib,

Sat Siri Akal. We are well and always wish for your wellbeing. Why do you delay writing letters? I feel upset that you have not sent any letter to me since arriving there.

Ask my friend Gurmeet Singh why he has not replied to my letter. Let me know if he is studying somewhere? Bibi Perminder Kaur has gone to Ramgarh. She will come here after 15-16 days when her school holidays start. Please send me 8 rupees. Chani stays at home and he talks a lot. At our house a little Guddi, a little baby [Gurmukh's second daughter] has arrived, she is a week old now. All her brothers and sisters are very happy.

From all of us, with folded hands a Sat Siri Akal to Jeeto, Pali [Kartar's nieces] and their Mama, Chacha [father].

Sat Siri Akal

Your loving son Balbir

From Gurmukh Singh, 10.8.1944, Lalheri

Dear brother Kartar Singh, Sat Siri Akal.

I am enclosing a copy of the letter MM wrote to me after receiving your wire.

They wrote that they will give the children all the help required. We will definitely take a copy of their letter with us to Bombay. As soon as they send a wire to us, I will take Angrez Kaur and kids straightaway to board the ship. Balbir's certificate will also be sent along with him. Let me know if you need anything else from here.

Kids are all well over here. Gurbachan Kaur [Gurmukh's wife] gave birth to a baby girl [Harminder] on 10th July, and they are both well.

From MM to Gurmukh Singh, 14.7.1944.

To Gurmukh Singh Sumal c/o M/s LalooRam, Ram Swaroop, Khanna

Dear Sir,

With reference to the correspondence ending with our letter of 22nd May 1944 and your reply regarding booking of passage for Mrs Kartar Singh Sumal and children we give below for your information a copy of telegram dated 6 July 1944 received by us from the General Manager, Kenya and Uganda Railways and Harbour, Nairobi.

"My telegram 26th April arrange passage second class for Mrs Kartar Sumal and children"

The passage for Mrs Kartar Singh Sumal and children, will therefore be arranged in second class. However, if second class accommodation is not available, they should be prepared to travel in deck class.

Due to war conditions and consequent shortage of accommodation we are not in a position at present to advise you when they will be called here for embarkation. As soon as accommodation becomes available, we will advise you on the date on which they should report here.

Every endeavor is being made to secure passage for them as early as possible.

Yours faithfully,
Mackinnon Mackenzie & co
Agent K.U.R Agents

From Gurmukh Singh, 27.10.1944, Lalheri

Dear brother Kartar Singh.

I received your money order for Rs 397. As per your instructions, I gave Rs 50 to Angrez Kaur and Rs 10 to Balbir Singh the same day. He has been fine for the last 3-4 months, which is really good news.

We have been ready to leave since receiving Mackinnon Mackenzie's letter on 2nd September. You have been feeling troubled waiting over there, but now this constant wait is troubling me too. I don't go anywhere knowing that they may call us at short notice. The disappointment carries on. Now, Binni's age is possibly over 3, so check about his ticket, unless you have already arranged it. Passports etc. are all with Mackinnon Mackenzie.

Write about your work. Are railways still recruiting people and have they employed anyone from India or is their recruitment only for people already residing there? Getting a job over here is very difficult, and both the Railways and Post Office have rejected my applications. I am considering joining the military over here if there is no other option.

Even Shangara Singh has been working on our farm since he returned from Simla. Our household expenses are very high, no less than Rs 100-150 per month, and income is low. It is difficult to make do, on just the income from our farmland.

The end of the war is not in sight. That is what worries me. Who knows how long it will carry on for. If it carries on for long, we might end up dying of hunger. I am in a quandary these days. My heart is in turmoil about my future and I feel helpless in these unsettled times. There is no-one to advise me, as to what will be best to do. Anyway, Waheguru [God] is our savior.

Don't worry at all about Angrez Kaur and the children. They are all hale and hearty. Balbir Singh and Barhi Guddi are on their school holidays. Chani misses you the most and remembers you all the time. Binni is also talking a lot and is perfectly healthy.

Your loving brother, Gurmukh Singh

Note:

The condition of our house is very bad at present. The cement on the floor is all cracking up and the doors and windows need painting. My plan is to get it repaired and painted and get the floor cemented, which will cost us Rs 80-100. Give me your opinion whether we should get these repairs done or not.

CHAPTER 3

1945
Unemployment and Inflation

Recollections of Kartar's son Chani (Harcharan)

I was two and a half years old when we left for India in 1942, so my memories are quite vague. I remember that I missed my dad (Kartar Singh) a lot and felt sad all the time. All I can remember about Bebeji, our grandmother, is that she had a very kind looking face. Two incidents from that time stand out in my mind.

With limited stimulation in the village, I often used to feel bored. As a four-year-old, I set off one day at dawn, in search of adventure. I asked a local shepherd named Kheru if I could accompany him and convinced him that my parents had given me permission. I thoroughly enjoyed the novelty of grazing sheep and goats for a couple of miles. But soon, hunger and tiredness set in, and the fun was over. So, I returned home, much to the relief of my distraught family, who had woken up to find me missing. This is the incident my cousin brother Kuldip (Nanhi) has referred to in one of the letters.

The other incident occurred when I rushed up the stairs to the rooftop of our Lalheri house, to run across a plank that was normally used to cross over to the neighboring house. Not knowing that my elder brother Balbir and cousin sister Baljeet had removed the plank, I jumped without looking, onto the nonexistent plank and went tumbling down from the roof, to land on top of an old plough covered

124

with thorny bushes. The shock of the fall knocked me out for a few minutes. When I slowly opened my eyes, I was astonished to find several panic-stricken eyes staring at me. I was lying in my Mama's lap and silent tears were flowing down her cheeks. I had injured my leg, but was fine otherwise.

I was fascinated by our farm animals in Lalheri. My favorite story at the time was about a buffalo that head-butted a goat. But sometimes I would say it the wrong way round, that the buffalo got head butted and cried "maah". Everyone laughed at my crazy story so I continued to repeat it all the time. I liked to imitate the sounds of our farm animals to entertain my audience, even after arriving in Kenya.

The letters of 1945 and 1946 focus on rising unemployment and inflation, leading to food shortages and struggles to feed the joint family, while trying to find alternative sources of income.

From Gurmukh Singh, 5.2.1945, Bombay

Dear brother Kartar Singh, Sat Siri Akal.

I left from Khanna on 2nd February and arrived in Bombay on Sunday 4 February. I met Mr Jeevan Singh at Lal Devi's house and mentioned about you. He said he has already been in correspondence with Mackinnon Mackenzie.

You wrote that Mantri is a clerk in the branch that books railways' passages, but I didn't go to him at all even though he tried to strike an acquaintance with me unnecessarily, perhaps to get something out of it. Mantri just deals with private passengers.

As instructed by Mr Jeevan Singh, I went to the Office of MM on Monday morning to see the Head Clerk Mr Uringa, and told him about the difficult situation we have been stuck in for a year. He seems very decent and talking to him face to face helped. I showed him all our correspondence and quietly mentioned to him that if he helps us, we will "look after him" and he understood what I meant.

He advised me to send the family by 1st class, the only tickets that are available. I told him we can't afford 1st class at Rs 465 per ticket. The total cost of Rs 1400 is beyond our reach. I arranged another meeting for the following day, when Mr Jeevan Singh accompanied me. I told him to try for 2nd class if there is no chance for deck tickets, which will make their journey easier and more comfortable. I think 2nd class costs Rs 260, which seems quite reasonable. There are several men staying in the same place as me, who have paid Rs 240 for a dhow ticket. Plus, they have to take their own rations/groceries with them on a dhow.

The Head Clerk didn't accept my offer to pay for tickets. He said when the General Manager confirms the passage, then they will sort out the payment with the railways in Kenya. He didn't commit to anything, but has promised to arrange passage after March, which I think will be half or full fare [code word for sweetener]. I will see him once again tomorrow and will let you know what his gesture implies. We will be given priority. Now, you don't worry at all. If there is any other important matter, Angrez Kaur will tell you herself in person, because my job is done today.

It is costly staying here, but I will have to stay another day to finalize this matter. Here in the hotel, my daily expense is Rs 4 (Rs 2 for bed & Rs 2 for roti/meal), but I try to make do with less than Rs 2 for roti. I have to confess that I traveled in inter-class on the train [Intermediate class, where 3rd class was provided with cushioned seats], and will return on it too, as it is less tiring than traveling in 3rd class where you often don't even get a seat to sit on. This extra Rs 10-20 can be added to my personal expenses. I have not done any extravagant spending like going to the cinema or staying in a better place.

Now, you don't worry about anything at all. It will all be arranged soon. You must keep all this information to yourself and don't mention it to anyone. I have also sent you a wire today because you must be eagerly waiting for news regarding the passage. Don't worry, if Waheguru permits, the children will hopefully be on the way by the end of March.

Now it is almost 11 o'clock at night so I will end here. Sat Siri Akal to you all.

Your loving brother, Gurmukh Singh, Bombay.

From Gurmukh Singh, 16.2.45, Lalheri

Dear brother Kartar Singh, Sat Siri Akal.

I gave Rs 50 in advance to Mackinnon Mackenzie for the fare [as a sweetener] and another 50 will be given when the task is accomplished. I cannot give

any more details but they have promised to do everything in their power to arrange a passage as early as
possible. Sardar Jeevan Singh has a good relationship
with those people, so it helped to have him with me.

Angrez Kaur, Chani and Binni went to Badochi with
Amar Singh [Angrez's brother], a few days ago. Barhi
Guddi is studying at Ramgarh and is well settled
there. Balbir Singh stayed at home due to his approaching examinations. Do not worry about anything
regarding Balbir Singh. With Waheguru's blessings
he has been completely healthy for the past 3 to 4
months.

Sat Siri Akal to everyone from all of us.

Your loving brother Gurmukh Singh.

From Gurmukh Singh, 24/5/45, Lalheri

Dear brother Kartar Singh.

Everything is fine here and we always ask Waheguru
for your wellbeing.

Shangara Singh returned yesterday morning after
seeing off Angrez Kaur and children in Bombay. I as-
sume you also received his telegram that very day. I
think that with Waheguru's blessings the children will
reach there without any problems. After all the hassle,
we finally managed to accomplish it in the end.

Love to all the children from all of us and Sat Siri Akal to both of you.

Your loving brother Gurmukh Singh.

From Kartar's daughter Perminder

None of us had any inkling that our four-month vacation would stretch to three years. Despite our priority as dad's dependents, it took us over two years after his departure, to get a passage on a ship. Uncle Shangara Singh accompanied us to Bombay. We were in a 'ladies only' coach but he came over to check on us at stations, and we all shared snacks which we had brought with us for the journey. He saw us off safely on board the ship.

The Railways covered deck class fares for us, so that is how we always traveled. We had to take our own roll up beddings and food/groceries. My brother Chani and I were sea sick throughout the ten-day long ship journey and felt so weak that our Mama had to carry us both to the bathroom. The only food we could digest was bread, so our ten-year-old elder brother Biri continued to buy it for us from the dining room. He helped Mama a lot by running errands while she looked after us and our little brother Binni.

When we landed at the coastal town of Mombasa, it felt like a homecoming, after three long years in India, during which we had really missed our dad. Waiting to disembark we saw a man in a white turban. Chani and I ran excitedly towards him, but felt crestfallen to learn he wasn't our dad. Our father arrived soon after, but we hesitated momentarily until we recognized his beaming smile, and rushed into his outstretched arms for long hugs.

On the train, we were very excited to see African huts and wild animals roaming freely, having forgotten all about them during our long stay in India. This was a new beginning for all of us and it felt wonderful to be together as a complete family at last.

From Gurmukh Singh, 25.12.1945, Lalheri

Dear brother Kartar Singh, Sat Siri Akal.

I was offered employment in the Principality of Bahawalpur [in Southern Punjab, now in Pakistan] which is approximately 40 miles further away from Multan. I did go there but had to return home feeling disappointed, after being offered very low wages. I might have managed on my own but wouldn't have survived on such low wages with my family over there.

After that I tried at Dept of Irrigation, Amritsar but a job in Government offices over here is impossible because they don't consider anyone with qualifications below matriculation [high school certificate]. Both Railways and the Post Office also rejected my applications. The Post Office refused me on the basis of being too old. I considered joining the military, but there was no-one to take care of my children if I left them behind.

Besides these discouraging attempts, I have been waiting for the permit from you, which it seems is not going to materialize, either. Shangara Singh is still unemployed,

As a last resort, I have agreed to start a shop with Gurdial Singh [a relative] and Puran Singh as partners. Gurdial Singh has paid my share of Rs 1000 for the partnership. It is in the old market in Khanna and the shop will stock fertilizer, cotton seeds, salt, rice, chane (chickpeas), savory snacks and also groceries like sugar, tea, soap etc.

It would have been better if I had started the shop straightaway after returning from my job [in Africa]. I would have earned Rs 3000 by now, during these 4-5 years of war. But I had no experience of this at that time and the thought never crossed my mind. Even now, the chance of it being a success is because Gurdial Singh has the knowledge and experience of running a shop.

Rs 500 is needed very soon as I have promised to pay Gurdial Singh within 10-15 days and the remaining Rs 500, at the beginning of March. If you can help me, then please send Rs 500 by cheque to Imperial Bank, Ludhiana. If for any reason you can't send the money, then let me know soon. I will put 5-7 bighas of land as collateral [for cash loan] and hopefully the money from that will suffice.

We are getting a new well installed. The Government of Punjab has passed a scheme of installing 5,000 wells in Punjab, and our application has been accepted. The government will pay one fifth of the total expense of installation. It will be ready in 3 months, making it easier to irrigate our land.

Write to me soon. Love to the children.

Your loving brother Gurmukh Singh, Lalheri, P.O Khanna

CHAPTER 4

1946
Financial Struggles

From Kartar's daughter Perminder

When we returned to Kenya in 1945, our father Kartar Singh had a railway quarter near the station and next to the railway headquarters building in Nairobi. These quarters consisted of just one row of houses, adjacent to "Italian War Prisoners" camp. We were told to stay away from the camp, but my brothers and I did go there once out of curiosity, to check out why we were forbidden. The prisoners were excited to see us and came over to the fence. They grinned and waved but we just ran back to our house.

Our house consisted of just one big room, with verandas at the front and back. The front veranda was enclosed, to convert it into a room. The backyard was full of flowers, and our dad had made a path leading to the kitchen, domestic help's room and toilet, which were at the rear of the yard. He must have been living there for a while, to have planted those flowers, which were in full bloom when we arrived. The backyard looked beautiful.

Our father's elder sister, Aunty Karam Kaur and her family were living there with him. They had moved from Kisumu, into rented accommodation at Nairobi, but after some problems with the landlord, they had moved in with our dad. Our second cousins Jagdev

133

and Sato from Kisumu were also staying at our house. I think they
might have moved to Nairobi for the better schools it offered. There
were altogether fourteen people living at our house. So, our home
in Nairobi was bursting at the seams, just like the Lalheri home in
India. Us cousins enjoyed having so many playmates, but our mothers
struggled with household chores while the fathers faced financial
difficulties with so many mouths to feed on low incomes, in both
Lalheri and Nairobi.

In the mid-forties our brother Balbir Singh went through a very
rough patch with frequent epileptic fits. Mama was pregnant with
Jaihind at the time so to give her a break, our father decided against
home birth. Jaihind, our fourth brother, was the only sibling born
in a hospital, in February 1946. Our dad heard about a German
medicine for epilepsy which was expensive but he continued to buy
it, even on his low salary. This medication for our elder brother
Balbir is mentioned in the letters.

From Gurmukh Singh, 25.2.1946, Lalheri

Dear brother Kartar Singh, Sat Siri Akal.

Here all is well and we always ask Waheguru for
your wellbeing.

I am writing this letter from the shop in Khanna,
which I have been operating since the 22nd of last
month. It is called Kenya Store. The rent is Rs 11
per month, with sales of 10 to 15 rupees. Hopefully
the business will start improving slowly and steadily.
Gurdial Singh has put stock worth Rs 1600 out of his
own pocket. When I started the business, I told him
that I will start contributing my share, on receipt of

rupees from Kartar Singh. Now, after waiting for a month and a half for the money to arrive from you, I have told him that I will not be able to continue as his partner for much longer. Never mind, changes have to be made according to circumstances. I will continue to help Gurdial Singh as he started this business mainly at my suggestion.

The main reason for starting work at the shop was that my children would be able to attend better schools in Khanna. And also, I thought that if my business slowly picks up and gets to a profitable stage, then in 5-7 years if you planned to move back home, then we would have our own fancy store, all spic-and-span, stocked up with nice things, and providing an up-to-date service. Also, I would have fulfilled this desire of mine to run a business. I thought, if not now, then in the future we can try this brainwave of mine. Anyway, a man desires one thing, but Parmatma [God] does something else. "Man proposes, God disposes."

For the past one and a half months, Shangara Singh has gone with his friend Surjan Singh to work at a mill in Barnala. He will return home in a fortnight when the work ceases. Give us news about Balbir Singh, as to how he is. How is your work progressing?

Your loving brother Gurmukh Singh, Kenya Store, Khanna, Ludhiana.

The following long letter reflects Gurmukh Singh's desire to maintain the family's prestige and status in the village while feeling under pressure to meet the debt obligations incurred by starting the shop in Khanna. A business, which he perhaps started in order to meet the daily needs of the family and to give himself a purpose in life. The mention of putting his share of the family land as collateral to borrow money, reflects his feelings of desperation and sad disappointment at feeling compelled by circumstances, to tarnish the family's well-to-do image in the village.

From Gurmukh Singh, 3.3.1946, Lalheri

Dear brother Kartar Singh, Sat Siri Akal.

After waiting for your letter for a long time. I wrote you another letter a week ago, full of the same old "ronha dhona" [lamenting & moaning] that I have written in the past.

If we had withdrawn our case against Sundar Singh [dispute over boundary with the farmer owning land adjacent to the brothers], then all our near ones in the village would have made life difficult for us. They would have said that the false pride of Africa wale [the family from Africa] has been revealed. After our initial defeat in Samrala we could not afford to remain silent, because it was a question of our prestige in the village, although the land itself is not of much value. Now, the judgment has been made in our favor in the appeal case at Ludhiana, although it cost us Rs 175-200.

The thinking is that Sundar will definitely lodge an appeal to Lahore High Court, which has to be done within 3 months. The judgment is expected to go in our favor but the expenses will be no less than Rs 200-300. If he appeals and we do not appear in court then that will also bring shame on us, that we were talking big but turned out to be just hollow inside. So, we definitely have to do it, to maintain our prestige, not just mine but of every one of you.

It has always been my consideration to not create any hardship for you. If I am upset and, in some difficulty, you will feel my hardship. In a joint family, the troubles of one are felt by the rest. If there is pain in the foot or a headache or a stomach ache then the whole body feels the effect. It cannot happen that there is a headache and the rest of the body is relaxed, because the head is not separate from the body. That will be so until the time we split up. The heavy load on you is felt and recognized by others even if they do not contribute financially. Do not think that we have discarded you away on your own.

In our country and our family, the joint family system still exists. According to my thinking I always have this belief that the joint family system is good despite the quarrels and friction within it. I understand what you have written about your need to provide for your family there. It is not like before when you were on your own and could save money and send it here. Do not mind me writing this, because we both know all about each other, because we are blood brothers and we have lived together at home and abroad.

Over the last few years Rs 1400 sent by you was spent on buying more land. That money was well invested and if it had remained invested in the land, that would have been very good and we would have managed financially to run the household, somehow or other. But by losing the land, and that too within

2-3 years, everything in the house has turned upside down. And for this I am even more saddened than you are.

Anyway, as far as I can, I will try my best to keep this household running until I come up against a brick wall and am unable to see any other options. The important thing is that you feel my pain and I feel yours. I feel more for your pain than my own, because you are my own blood, and it is not good if an unfair advantage is taken of you.

You don't have anything to give at present and I trust and believe everything you have written in your letter. Such is our fate, that you are facing even more difficulties than us, and I really feel for you going through a difficult time. You have written about the extra expenses incurred due to Balbir Singh's illness, and even then, he is not improving.

You have written about our land's mukhtarnama [Power of attorney]. After the harvesting period ends in May, I can request for your share to be put up as collateral land. But first, I will put my share up as collateral land, for a cash loan [to be forfeited in the event of default]. If this does not suffice, then we will look at your share too. At present, your gesture of offering your share of the land as collateral, is more than enough. Until now, people have believed that we are rich but when we put our land up as collateral then this belief will be broken. Now it is a matter of jhoothi shaan [false pride].

I didn't think obtaining a permit for Kenya would have taken so long and I am glad that you are working hard to get permits for both of us. Shangara Singh returned home yesterday, after working for two months. He is well and will write to you himself about his thoughts.

I am very happy to hear the news that Angrez Kaur has given birth to a boy (Jaihind). May Waheguru give him a long life.

Everyone over here is well. Bebeji's health is not too good. She might improve now, with warmer weather. Sat Siri Akal to both of you from all of us and love to the children. Reply soon, and don't delay - this is my request.

As always, your brother Gurmukh Singh, Kenya Store.

RECEIPTS FOR MONEY TRANSFERRED FROM KENYA TO INDIA

From Shangara Singh, 3.3.1946, Lalheri

Dear brother Kartar Singh, Sat Siri Akal.

I learnt from your letter that there is no improvement in Balbir Singh's [Kartar's eldest son] health. I do not understand why no medicine is working.

Gurmukh Singh must have already told you everything about the circumstances at home and I have nothing to add. I am trying very hard to find work, I will do any job, whatever they pay, as it is difficult staying idle at home.

We have received an invitation from Badochi, for the wedding of Mukhtiar (Angrez Kaur's sister). Bebeji's health is as before, she is sick more often than well.

Sat Siri Akal from all of us to all of you.

Your loving brother, Shangara Singh

From Gurmukh Singh, 8.4.1946, Lalheri

Dear brother Kartar Singh, Sat Siri Akal.

I received your letter dated 21.3.46, along with your money order for Rs 100, which will be of great help. After reading your letter, I am more worried about you than about myself.

I am most worried about Balbir Singh's health, because here I saw him having a 15 minute long fit and quite often, he would have 5-6 fits in one day and night. At that time, I could not bear to see his condition. Aziz [Dear] Balbir Singh's health is a constant worry.

Shangara Singh along with Nanhi [his son] went to Badochi, for the wedding, so he will give you all the news in his letter.

The main difficulty at present, is obtaining a permit (for Kenya). I know you have been trying hard, without any success. If we get the permits then perhaps, we can both come together, and our families can come later. One day we have to get out of this home, whether alone or together.

And I think, instead of railways, a job with a private firm will be good too. I will learn typing and book-keeping as these certificates will help me to find a job with a firm. On railways' wages it is difficult to survive with a family, unless you are a Guard. Their starting wage is probably not more than 150. There is no worry about Shangara Singh because he will probably get a job soon after arriving [it was easier for skilled workers to get a job].

We are very happy to hear about the birth of Kaka [baby boy, Jaihind]. Let us know of Angrez Kaur and Kaka's health. Tell Chani that his black chheli (goat), which was about to give birth, died. She was very healthy but her still born baby goat caused complications and her death too. She was worth at least Rs 50.

As always, your brother Gurmukh Singh, Kenya Store, Khanna.

From Gurmukh Singh, 21.5.1946, Lalheri

Dear brother Kartar Singh, Sat Siri Akal

I received your letter dated 4.5.46 today and am very happy to read that my permit has been accepted. I will start my preparations without any delay. Passport renewal will take two months, during which time I will do my typing course at Ludhiana. I will also get two certificates from shopkeepers in Khanna, stating that I have worked as a salesman.

Regarding Shangara Singh's permit, if you are unsuccessful in Kenya, then try in Uganda. This is my special request, that you keep trying your best to get it at any cost, so that both of us can come together by August. I am not worried about his job because as an electrician there will be opportunities in Nairobi. I hope that by then you will be able to give some help towards his fare, but if you can't afford to send any rupees then I will somehow arrange something over here.

You have written that to qualify for a permit, a person must have resided there for at least 5 years, but I don't think that is true. Some people have got permits as first-time visitors [these permits might have been for people with special skills].

What you have written about me coming alone, I don't think there is any other option as the remaining three tickets will cost Rs 800. Until one of our men comes from Africa to take my family, they will have to live here, in whatever condition it is, good or bad. They won't have a choice. If Shangara Singh's permit can be arranged, we can come together, and Gurbachan Kaur & Jaswant Kaur [their wives] can come later.

You must have read in papers regarding "Hindustan and Jaihind" [India and Long Live India]. This is a very good thing.

From all of us Sat Siri Akal to both of you and love to the children.

As always, your brother Gurmukh Singh.

Note: Kartar obtained a job offer letter for Gurmukh Singh from his friend Mohinder Singh's father, Ishar Singh Pakharpuria who owned a carpentry shop and could recruit carpenters from India. Gurmukh's job offer was as a carpenter, a reserve category for which immigration restrictions were slowly being lifted. Gurmukh's previous stay in Kenya for more than five years also helped his case. Using this letter of a job offer, Kartar was able to get a "Special Endorsement Certificate" by paying a deposit of 685 shillings to be refunded after one year of useful employment in Kenya.

From Gurmukh Singh, 15.6.1946, Lalheri

Dear Brother Kartar Singh Ji, Sat Siri Akal.

I am learning typing and bookkeeping at Commercial College, Ludhiana, and will complete the course on

144

August 15. The fee is Rs 10 per month. Rs 15 were spent on books and note books. During weekdays I stay in Ramgarh and cycle to Ludhiana and back, to attend classes. The cycle journey is difficult and we are required to do typing and bookkeeping from morning until evening, but I think these two certificates will help me to get employment in Kenya.

Both Mackinnon McKenzie and Smith & Mackenzie have rejected my request for an early passage, because they already have a lot of prior bookings on their waiting list. I have now requested MM to book my passage by early September and to register my family's names along with mine. I have promised to pay them in advance upon confirmation of passage, which will give us more certainty.

Initially it did not seem right to bring my family along and until now this was not my plan but now, I have decided to bring them with me, for reasons best known to me only.

Jaswant Kaur [Shangara Singh's wife] is expecting a baby within a month, so she will be fit to travel by early September. I will make some sort of arrangements here, but I have nothing except a Singer Sewing machine that I can sell for up to Rs 175-200. Put aside whatever you can afford to send to me from June's pay.

Write about Balbir Singh's health. From all of us Sat Siri Akal to both of you and lots of love to the children.

Your loving brother Gurmukh Singh, Lalheri, Post Office Khanna, District Ludhiana.

Note: It must have been heartbreaking for Kartar and Angrez to see their first born in a helpless condition of continued epileptic fits, with no cure in sight. Working long hours to meet the needs for Balbir's treatment, the hospital bill for Jaihind's birth and financial needs of the family in India must have taken a toll on Kartar's mental state. These dark feelings of helpless anguish and despair were probably reflected in the letter Kartar wrote to Gurmukh.

From Gurmukh Singh, 25.9.1946, Lalheri

Dear brother Kartar Singh

I received Rs 200 from you, followed by your letter a few days later telling us that you are going through a very difficult time. So much so, that after sending us Rs 200, you had reached a point of ending your life. I was very saddened to hear this. If you were in such difficulty then you should not have sent the rupees. I would have managed somehow or other, but I do not want to see you in distress. Every moment of the day, I also think of one thing and that is Aziz Balbir Singh's illness.

You had sent Rs 200 for my fare but I used it to pay for the new well instead because that matter was more pressing.

Our updated passports were received two weeks ago. A delay was caused by a month-long postal strike and secondly, I had to return Gurbachan Kaur's [his wife's] passport twice. Once, to get the little baby girl's name endorsed, who is two and a half months old now (Updesh). She was born on July 15, 1946. During her birth Gurbachan Kaur almost died as her heart started to fail and she was having convulsions. A doctor from Khanna came and gave her some medicine, which slowly made her better. The second time her passport had to be returned to Lahore due to a wrong expiry date. It is good that we noticed this official error in time, otherwise we would have had to return from Bombay. Now passports, vaccinations and all certificates are ready.

Reference our passage, you know yourself how difficult it was when we were trying for Angrez Kaur. That was being done through railways whereas this is a private application. Both Mackinnon Mackenzie and Smith & Mackenzie have given their standard reply "We cannot give guarantees and you will get seats when it is your turn."

I will arrange my fare myself, so you don't need to worry about it.

I have now got my certificate for typing and book-keeping, which will help me with my employment. My typing speed is slow at present but with practice it will get better.

Jaswant Kaur [Shangara Singh's wife] has a 15 days old baby girl (Khushdev). Bebeji has been very ill for the last ten days and her condition is bad due to weakness. Depending on her health, I might have to delay my departure.

Waheguru will do everything well.

As always, your brother Gurmukh Singh.

1st Postcard: From Gurmukh Singh,
21.11.1946, Lalheri

Dear brother Kartar Singh. May you have a long life, Sat Siri Akal.

The day after I wrote to you, Mackinnon Mackenzie from Bombay, wrote to say that "Our company has removed two ships from this line, and only two are operating now, so now your turn will come at the end of December or in January."

Bebeji's health is the same and the hope of her getting better is fading because she is very weak after being ill for over two months.

Write soon to let us know about Aziz Balbir Singh's health. Sat Siri Akal to you both from all of us, and love to children.

Gurmukh Singh, Lalheri, Zilla Ludhiana.

2nd Postcard: From Gurmukh Singh, 30.12.1946, Lalheri.

Dear brother Kartar Singh, Live long, Sat Siri Akal

The news is that despite our efforts, Bebeji's health is the same as before and there is no improvement due to her weakness and the very cold weather.

I have received a telegram from Bombay to say the ship will depart on 9th or 10th January. I will leave from home on January 4th, 1947. I will send you a letter or telegram from Bombay. I hope you will get leave for 1 or 2 days to enable you to come to Mombasa. The rest, we will talk when we are together. All at Ramgarh, Badochi are well. Love to kids

Your loving brother, Gurmukh Singh.

CHAPTER 5

1947
India's Independence and a Bloody Partition

After the departure of Gurmukh for Kenya, their younger brother Shangara took over the reins and shouldered responsibilities for the family left behind in India. To add to the difficulties of food shortages, inflation, limited income and a sick mother, there was now the looming danger of communal riots in the area. The letters of 1947 capture his personal soul-destroying experiences of the horrors of India's bloody partition into two countries - India and Pakistan.

From Gurmukh, 7.1.1947 Bombay (post card)

Dear Brother Kartar Singh, Sat Siri Akal.

Yesterday on 6/1/47, I along with the children reached Bombay. Today I got our tickets etc. and so far, everything has gone smoothly. I left home in sad circumstances, feeling worried about our Bebeji's condition, firstly her illness and secondly her lack of relief from pain. I do not know what the situation will be, with her health not improving and there is very little hope that I will meet her again in my life.

The expectation is that we will be on the ship Karanja sailing on 10/1, though there may be a delay of a day or two. People have been waiting here since the 1st. I think the ship will dock on the 20th/21st, so come to Mombasa, if you are able to.

As always, your brother Gurmukh Singh.

From Kartar's daughter Perminder

When Uncle Gurmukh Singh and family arrived in Kenya in January 1947, they stayed with us but I do not have much recollection of that period. I remember more about their stay with us later on when Uncle was transferred from Kisumu to Nairobi.

Our dad Kartar Singh had bought 6 comfortable arm-chairs in 1945, and later gave two to Uncle Gurmukh Singh and two to Uncle Shangara Singh, after they had settled in Kenya. I always admired this concept of sharing whatever little the Sumal brothers possessed.

From Shangara, 24.1.1947, Lalheri

Dear Brothers Gurmukh Singh and Kartar Singh, Sat Siri Akal.

On the day of Lohri [an Indian festival], Bebeji was remembering you a lot, saying that they must be celebrating by cooking kheer [rice pudding] on the ship. The sweater which Ghoge (Updesh) had outgrown, has been passed down to Choti Guddi (Khushdev) to wear. Everybody has started to call her Doddo.

After your departure I feel very alone. The responsibilities on my shoulders have doubled. The whole
night passes in worry. What more can I write? I do
not feel at ease at home or outside. I will keep doing
what everyone wants me to do. I do not understand
what is happening here. My heart itself does not
feel right, what more can I say to anyone? It feels as
if some big heavy stone has been placed on it. My
brain has become like that of a mad person and is
not functioning at all. I started to write a letter 2-3
times but could not continue.

Your brother, Shangara Singh.

After arriving in Kenya Gurmukh got a job in the "Public Works Department" to work in Kijabe, as a guard on trains transporting material for
the realignment of the railway line on the Eastern slope of the Rift Valley
(Kijabe to Longonot).

After working for about a month in Kijabe, Gurmukh got a temporary
job with the railways in Nakuru. He did odd jobs in the goods shed until he
was employed as a yard foreman there.

From Gurmukh Singh, 27.2.1947, Kijabe (Kenya)

Dear brother Kartar Singh, Sat Siri Akal.

I learnt while I was in Nairobi that the railway job
here is just for two months, but decided to come to
Kijabe to ascertain the exact position. This is what I
learned on arriving here:

It will take about three weeks for the railway line to
get to Longonot. After that they might dismiss me.

So, there is no point in bringing my family here just for a month or two.

I met with the supervisor and told him "I came here under the impression that this job was for two months but now I am being told that it is only for a month."

His reply was that this is definitely a temporary job but he couldn't say much more.

I am now in a very awkward position. It is an easy and good job with a good salary of 484 shillings [350 shillings plus 134], but there is the uncertainty. The notice period here has also been reduced from one month to only one week.

I have written a letter to Mr Mir Abdullah (supervisor at Nairobi railway station) this morning asking for other possibilities for a job. Go to his office on Saturday without fail and find out from him what his decision is.

Perhaps, it is better not to get Guddi [his eldest daughter Jasminder] admitted to school until we come to some decision about my work. You must have enjoyed your leave with all the children and with Waheguru's mercy all must be well.

Your loving brother Gurmukh Singh.

From Gurmukh Singh, 19.4.1947 Nakuru (Kenya)

Dear brother Kartar Singh, Sat Siri Akal.

My friend Laxman Singh and I are on different shifts so we are able to share one bed, in turns. On work days I come home at 10 o'clock and then cook my meal. For this reason, I have very limited interaction with anyone. Laxman is visiting Nairobi. I think I left my beard brush on the shoe shelf, so please send it with him and also 4 packets of butter, if you can, as I do not have any.

I have made an application for a job here and they are asking for 200 shillings [could be talking of paying a sweetener for a job]. Upon receiving the money, I will hand it in but please send the money as early as possible. I will repay the shillings when I get my pay. This month I bought a sack of flour, so I will send to you whatever I can manage.

News from India is very worrying [about communal riots]. We do not know what will happen to our family in India.

Sat Siri Akal to both of you, love to all the children

Your loving brother Gurmukh Singh

From Shangara Singh, 25.4.1947, Lalheri

Dear brothers Gurmukh Singh and Kartar Singh, Sat Siri Akal.

Bebeji's condition is the same as when you left, no better or worse. The doctor says that only an X-ray will give a diagnosis of her illness, so I will get it done

when there is some respite from communal disturbances. My condition is a lot better than before, so
don't worry about me. There is nothing to worry about
the situation at home. Whatever Waheguru wishes
will happen in the future.

The wheat harvesting is going ahead in full force because we want to get it done soon and stored indoors
safely. We have to watch out as many fields have
been burnt, due to communal riots. Our area is calm
so far but the danger is always there. I witnessed a
farmer's whole harvest being burnt to ashes, near
Ramgarh. There is no guarantee of life over here. Recently a man's Tanga [horse drawn passenger cart]
was attacked when he got caught in the riots in Ludhiana but luckily, he managed to escape unharmed.
The situation is bad, people are abandoning their
homes with nothing but the clothes they are wearing.
Thank God our area is peaceful so far.

The cow stopped producing milk but will hopefully
start producing it in 2 months when she is due to give
birth. On top of this, we could not buy any milk for
one week due to shortage. The children go without
milk and we have to manage with what little we have.
Buying a cow or a buffalo is expensive, so we might
look for a goat instead.

The man we sold our oxen to in Khanna, treated it
badly so I was compelled to buy it back for Rs 32 as
people had started saying that he would end up in a
slaughterhouse. Now his condition is improving and
he is working alongside the calf.

Chacha Perumal has got himself a woman, through
an agent. Her appearance is not very good, her age is
much advanced, and she is as tall as Bhai Tarkhan.
She speaks a different language. I heard that she had
a son and a daughter but she did not bring any children with her. Chacha has deferred the payment for
her until after the harvesting. The agent is threaten-
ing to take her away if he doesn't receive a payment.
Let's hope now that she does not run away with all
the kitchen utensils.

Sat Siri Akal to all of you and love to children from
Bebeji and me.

Your loving brother Shangara Singh.

From Gurmukh Singh, 12.5.1947, Nakuru

Dear brother Kartar Singh, Sat Siri Akal.

Write about how your interview went. I expect it went
well [interview for promotion to a Guard].

I am sending 11 shillings for the butter as you also
have a great need. Everything else is fine. Until now I
have been working in the goods shed but in the future
whatever Waheguru wishes will happen.

Sat Siri Akal to both of you from us and love to all
children.

Your brother Gurmukh Singh.

From Shangara Singh, 23.5.1947, Lalheri

Brothers Gurmukh Singh & Kartar Singh Ji, Sat Siri Akal.

I am sending the result of Bebeji's X-ray taken in Ludhiana. She has Tuberculosis and it has spread to both her lungs. I might get another X-ray done to confirm this result. Then we will try to get some treatment started. The pain is there most of the time, but the level fluctuates. The doctor recommended nutritional food, which is a problem due to shortage of milk or ghee/butter at home. There is no milk at all at home and we are continuing to make do without it. Kids are having to go without milk. The cow has not started producing milk yet and we don't know when she will give birth.

There is no doubt that you are missing us and are feeling unsettled, but the situation here is even worse, because your departure has had a big effect on everyone. Bebeji misses you and the children all the time but considering what your situation was over here, it is good that you have gone. However, you have left me facing a huge mountain here.

In areas around our village things are quiet but people are feeling very scared. Communal riots are still ongoing in big cities.

Your loving brother, Shangara Singh.

From Shangara Singh, 11.7.1947, Lalheri

Brothers Gurmukh Singh & Kartar Singh, Sat Siri Akal.

We started the reading of the Sikh holy book in the main hall, after getting it painted and properly cleaned. The bhog [completion ceremony of the reading of the holy book] was on July 7th. At the end of the bhog, the decision was made to arrange ishnaan [holy bath] at Haridwar for Bebeji's sharaad [paying homage to one's dead parents], because nobody knows how long she will live. It was Bebeji's desire because she felt that it might help her to get better. So yesterday four of us returned after having ishnaan [bath] in the holy water.

We will go to Patiala in 2-4 days for another X-ray and I will send you the result. We are taking a lot of precautions, but you can't keep kids from wandering near Bebeji. The temperature this summer has reached record levels, and in the absence of a cool breeze, we have to place Bebeji in water to cool her down, and ease her breathing. She is a bit better and is walking about a little but is still very weak.

Our cow gave birth to a calf yesterday so the milk supply will improve for a short period. The buffalo is close to giving birth.

The arguments over land consolidation are still continuing amongst the villagers.

As always, your loving brother Shangara Singh

From Shangara Singh, 3.8.1947, Lalheri

Dear brother Kartar Singh, Sat Siri Akal.

I am troubled and worried about Bebeji's illness. I do not go out anywhere even for a day or two because Bebeji doesn't want me out of her sight. She says she doesn't know how long she will live, although we haven't told her the details of her illness. She does not eat solid food and just drinks milk three times a day. The doctor's treatment has ended, so we will try homeopathic medicine now.

What happened regarding your promotion to a Guard?

Message from Nanhi (Shangara's son) to Chani (Kartar's son) "Do you get a chance to graze goats in Africa or not?"

This is Bebeji's report, if you want a second opinion:

X-RAY RESULTS - 1/4/04 to 15/7/1947:

Both upper lobes (infraclavicular regions) show small spotted and striped opacities. Heart and diaphragm are normal.

Conclusion: Bilateral pulmonary Tuberculosis

Your loving brother, Shangara Singh

India's Independence at the Cost of Pain & Suffering

At the end of World War II, an economically weakened Britain realized that it could no longer hold on to the jewel in its imperial crown, and stated that India would be free from British rule on August 15, 1947. It was also decided that with independence, India would have partition between the Hindu India and the Muslim Pakistan. Punjab and Bengal were the states to be divided primarily on the basis of religious demographics.

The task of demarcating the boundary was given to a British lawyer, Sir Cyril Radcliffe, who had never been to India. This "random line" partition triggered riots, mass casualties, and a colossal wave of migration, with millions of Muslims heading towards Pakistan, and Hindus and Sikhs in the direction of India. The chaos, violence and bloodshed escalated to horrendous levels and affected people on both sides.

Approximately 14.5 million people were displaced and up to a million people lost their lives. People had to leave the homes where their families had lived for generations. A countless number of women were kidnapped and raped brutally and then murdered. Their families were killed in front of them. Years later, charities were set up to repatriate the abducted women. Some of them were well settled in their new families by then and had children. They were often returned to their families against their wishes. Some families refused to accept them back, due to fear of social stigma.

Shangara lived in a part of Punjab where Sikhs outnumbered Muslims so the cruelty, he witnessed was more one-sided, where Muslims were the victims and the Sikhs, the perpetrators. The picture was reversed in the other half of Punjab, which became a part of Pakistan. Deep and uncontrollable feelings of hateful revenge led to brutal atrocities on both sides of the partition line. Although this painful period only lasted three months, other ramifications of this haphazard split in a country, continue to this day. It would be wrong to ignore and cruel and inhumane to justify that horrific and tragic chapter in Indian history.

The following heart wrenching letters capture the dark period of partition, as personally witnessed by Shangara. One can feel the raw pain, suffering and confusion in his mind. The majority of people like him were reduced to helplessly witnessing a small minority taking revenge in the most brutal manner on their neighbors and friends, leaving pain and sorrow in hearts of both the victims and bystanders.

During the riots, Shangara hid Muslim families in their house, to protect them from massacre. He saved the lives of their muslim farm worker Babu, his brother and their families. Babu's nieces called Amna and Shamna were still there in Lalheri, in 1963/64, when the three Sumal brothers moved back home, to spend their retirement in India.

From Shangara Singh, 29.9.1947, Lalheri

Dear brothers Gurmukh Singh ji and Kartar Singh ji, Sat Siri Akal.

The postal service was shut down for a long time. Today, we have finally started to plow the farmland. There has been a curfew since the beginning of August, so anyone who went outdoors was fined. We could only go to the farm to fetch the greens for our cattle. There were guards all around the village. In Khanna and the surrounding villages, there was a lot of security, thanks to Mohinder Singh of Iron Mills. Whenever he got just a little whiff of information about any attack, he arranged for the soldiers to appear there. Soldiers were present outside our house day and night, otherwise there was no hope of being saved.

Every village had set up its own alarm system. We set up an alarm bell on our roof top, and sounded it whenever there was news of an attack, to warn people to assemble in a designated safe place. Now if Nanhi and Lakha [Shangara's two sons] hear an alarm, even for no reason, they say "Hide quickly, the Muslims are coming." Schools are all shut down. Nanhi's muslim teacher has left for Pakistan but I don't know whether he reached there safely.

May Waheguru prevent us from ever seeing such dark days again. When the sun set, people went in groups towards the farm to defecate. We could see the dead bodies of men, women and children everywhere. People dragged the bodies as if they were stray dogs and piled them up in heaps. It is difficult to comprehend and describe the images.

Muslims from our village and the surrounding areas have left with whatever belongings they could carry. The belongings and cattle left behind by them were looted and their houses are now lying vacant. There are still incidents of Muslims being attacked and killed, after being spotted hiding in the sugarcane crop. One such incident occurred near us. It is a long story and it is not possible to write about every incident.

Muslim skilled workers like carpenters and black-smiths have left along with their families and have not been seen since. Muslims that were found hiding in odd villages, were also cleared out. Now no Muslims are around, none to dye clothes, none to fit "Khuria" [horseshoes], no vegetable vendors. We got news that Muslims from our area, Bagga, Chondha, Baksh, have all been killed by Sikhs from Sirhind and its surrounding villages.

Bhattia, Akalai have become Sikhs and they have turned a mosque into a Sikh temple. In our village a clan of Muslims has returned after converting to Sikhs. The rest, like Yusuf & his family, Wazir's family, tailor Bakshi, were all killed by the Sikh groups. The ones that survived over here, have all become Sikhs, and are living at our Gurudwara [temple] now, which Bhai Miya Singh has got ready, with Waheguru's mercy. Only those Muslims that the villagers had kept protected, by converting them to Sikhs, are left in every village. They are in small numbers of between five and seven, people who did not wish to go to Pakistan.

Displaced Muslims had assembled in enclaved villages. They were armed and started retaliating. Near Ramgarh, Muslims attacked houses of Sikh farmers, killing 30 people. Sanjhi [sharecropper] Sattu of Ramgarh, and his brother were killed. Our brother-in-law, Sucha Singh kept watch with his binoculars. Sikhs armed with weapons patrolled around their village. On learning that 4000 Muslims had gathered in a nearby village, all the children from Ramgarh were brought to Lalheri, as Ramgarh was in grave danger.

Now, the danger has increased for us, no-one dares to go out after sunset. A loud alarm, a microphone and a loudspeaker were installed at the Gurudwara. Maan Singh brought his own generator and batteries to supply electricity to the surrounding four Gurudwaras. Information about possible attacks were announced on Gurudwara loudspeakers. On hearing this, people assembled in the Gurudwara [Sikh temple] for safety. Our Gurudwara has helped a lot in saving people's lives.

With Waheguru's mercy, we might meet again if our lives are saved. For 48 hours we didn't even get a chance to cook any food. All women and children were kept enclosed and hidden in the center of the village and four men were left there permanently to guard them. We have been spending day and night guarding our farmlands. Kids were crying, asking us to save our possessions, and they are still waking up, feeling scared from nightmares.

In our village, where no money could ever be collected for anything, a total sum of Rs 2000 was collected for the security of the community. Every house, even while putting up with shortages, contributed Rs 100 each. People in the village had bought illegal pistols for their protection. Anyway, we had to face very horrifying dangers, and who knows 'kis kutton ke muh par parhe hotey' [where we would have ended up] if we had not organized our security. In olden times people used to say that dogs and vultures do not eat human flesh, but in our fields, we saw them feeding on dead humans as if they were cattle.

[Barr, mentioned in the following paragraph, was a fertile area in North Western Punjab, now Pakistan, which was irrigated by British built canals. Farms in the area were sold to the general public and also given as a reward to Indians who had served in the British army. A large number of Sikh farmers in Eastern Punjab, India sold their lands and moved to the Barr area].

None of our people from Barr have arrived except for the ones who left before August 15th (Independence Day). Many of our people have come in the Multan Kafila [caravan or foot column from Multan in Pakistan] but none from Natha Singh's family have arrived yet. They may come in the other two Kafilas, unless they have been killed there. We still need to make further enquiries about our acquaintances who have not arrived yet, like Sadhu, Abbasa and Puru Choora's (sweeper caste) brother Pura.

KAFILA (CARAVAN OR FOOT COLUMN) DURING INDIA'S PARTITION AFTER INDEPENDENCE

Two days ago, I went to Amritsar to help people from our area coming across the border and learnt that one Kafila had arrived in Ferozepur on oxen carts. Three Kafilas are coming from Kila Multana. People in thousands arrive from Pakistan villages via Ferozepur, loaded on oxen carts, with their weapons. People from the Lahore district are coming on trains, and are in greater danger, because many on the trains are being killed on the way. Women are having to leave their children behind and escape. People leaving from Lahore are searched, as they can bring no possessions or money. They have shut all the taps, and are going to the extent of not allowing even drinking water.

Arriving on the Indian side of the border, refugees gather in camps, from where the Indian army takes them in trucks to other destinations in India, some keep going on foot, escorted by the army. Indian airplanes have started dropping food for our camps. The Kafilas from Pakistan are so long that it took one of them 36 hours to cross a river bridge, and another one took 24 hours. People have arrived in their lakhs [hundred thousand], loaded in trains and on foot. The number of dead is also very high.

Passengers on trains travel free, no fare is collected. Only a few passenger trains have been running for a month, so people are traveling on goods trains, sitting on the roofs, in their thousands. There are more people on the roofs than inside. Thousands travel on every train, along with all their possessions including beds, everything on the train's roof. The world has never seen anything like this.

LOADED TRAINS DURING INDIA'S PARTITION AFTER INDEPENDENCE

Gurdial Singh's relatives had arrived from Pakistan so he went to Amritsar to fetch them. They could not bring anything with them except for some bedding and a few kitchen utensils. Shangar Singh's whole family has arrived, except for his daughter and son-in-law who converted to Muslims and stayed behind in Pakistan. They have applied to the Military for assistance because the military is trying to get those men and women who have converted to Muslim religion, out of Pakistan. All of Sher Singh's family has arrived, and I took them to their home the day before yesterday. People who have arrived have nothing left besides their lives. With Waheguru's grace the situation is much better now and the danger that was surrounding us from all four sides is over.

The vacated Muslim houses will be allocated by the government to the people who have come from Barr. No person has settled in our village yet. It has been announced that people from districts Lyallpur and Rawalpindi, will be settled in our district, Ludhiana. Refugees in huge numbers are sitting around at train stations and they cannot get any food. There is a langar [free meals served by Sikhs] but even then, there is difficulty.

My heart cries all the time, wondering whether Waheguru will enable us to meet again or not. I am surrounded by difficulties on all sides. I had arranged to start work at Saharanpur but then the disturbances began, and it was not possible to go out. Now all the work and businesses have shut down. I digress, a request to you and brother Kartar Singh to let me know how to organize everything about urgently needed house repairs, otherwise Waheguru is my savior. One never knows when adversity will strike.

Your brother, Shangara Singh

MAP OF PUNJAB HIGHLIGHTING THE TOWNS MENTIONED IN THE LETTERS

From Shangara Singh, 25.10.1947, Lalheri

Brothers Gurmukh Singh & Kartar Singh Ji, Sat Siri Akal.

I wrote to you previously, but will give you more details about the situation over here after August 15th [India's Independence Day].

Our town's Maulwi's [Muslim Priest] brother was killed before he could reach Pakistan's border. The Sikh owner of Iron Mills in Khanna, lent his car and

driver to the Maulwi and his friend, to visit the area
where his brother was killed but the car returned
without them. They were both killed on the way, as
a result of which, the strong Muslim influence in
Khanna was significantly reduced.

After Maulwi's death, his son-in-law Ibrahim was
next on the hit list. On August 23rd, he was shot as
he stepped out from his house. The news of the attack spread quickly by word of mouth amongst the
rest of the Muslim community. They carried him to
the hospital, where a Hindu doctor treated him and
released him later. In the meantime, Sikhs from the
surrounding areas had gathered outside the hospital
with one purpose in mind, to kill him. So as soon as
he stepped out, the Sikhs ambushed him and killed
him. Somehow, this made the Sikhs feel they were
in control.

Soon afterwards, one of the neighboring villages was
attacked by Muslims, but the villagers were saved
by gathering at the Gurudwara. Luckily for them,
the pistols of Muslims shooting from their trucks did
not work. After the attack, a group of us went to
Mohinder Singh of the Iron Works to ask for help.
He accompanied us to the police station to ask for
ammunition and protection. The policemen told us
to gather together spears, swords etc. and arrange
to stay on guard. He said if we want pistols, then by
the time our application for a license is accepted, this
whole game will be over. Mohinder Singh decided to
gather as many volunteers as possible to form a jatha
[vigilantes] to attack the Muslims. While we were
sitting there, he got everything organized and made

preparations to execute the planned attack within 2 hours, at 4 pm. The group included 6 men with 'lohe ke kapde' [iron armor] and they went straight to the Muslim enclave that had attacked our Gurudwara with guns. Eventually the fighting intensified and the village was set on fire. A countless number of men and women were killed, I can't say how many. Very few came out alive. People started looting the houses. Taps and doors, along with their wooden framework were pulled out and taken away.

Hearing about this incident Muslims in two other enclaves nearby felt terrified, knowing that they were next in line for an attack. So, they fled in different directions and some got killed. Others who survived went to Ambala refugee camp.

The Military, which was stationed at A.S School in Khanna said they would go out to patrol the surrounding areas for three hours, implying that during that period, the citizens were free to do whatever they wanted to do in our town [turn a blind eye]. After the military returned from their patrol, not a single Muslim was left alive, be it vegetables wala, clothes wala or cloth dyers. They were all killed. Our Muslim family friends, acquaintances, and all Muslim shopkeepers and traders that we knew, were all there at the time. We learnt later that only Muslims who had left town very early in the morning escaped safely, the rest were all killed. There were around ten dead bodies lying in each house. Khanna was emptied of Muslims. Khanna was looted and parts of it burnt to ashes.

On hearing the news of a deserted Khanna, Muslims from our village and surrounding villages, who were hiding in the farms left in a hurry. They took their belongings and some took their cattle with them. Our villagers were sitting prepared on their rooftops and doorways, fearing a Muslim counter attack. From our rooftop, we could see it all, the fires and smoke rising over Khanna. We will not forget those days throughout our lives. In fact, not just us but our future generations too will not forget such dark days.

In September the fighting moved to other surrounding areas where people were killed in thousands and dragged like dogs to make piles of hundreds. After it was over, the thanedar [man in charge of the Police Station] came and ordered people to pile up the dead bodies and burn them. These piles of bodies were set on fire, after sprinkling oil and piling wood on top. Dogs ate a lot of the dead bodies, as did vultures. Ancient people used to say a vulture does not eat human flesh but I happened to witness such scenes where it was difficult to even pause for a minute. I witnessed humanity in its lowest form. Children were lying dead, clinging to their dead mothers' bosoms. Some had been burnt while they were still alive. I saw a pile of 60-70 bodies being set on fire. I saw a woman being burnt alive. They had removed her clothes before placing her alive on the fire.

Afterwards Sikhs gathered the Muslim girls and removed their clothes. They were made to stand naked on one side in a gathering of thousands. Those who agreed to become Singhni [wife], were told to stand on one side. Some of the jathe wale men [Sikhs]

took them to their homes. The rest, the ones who
didn't agree to become their wives, were dishonored
and killed. In all the history that I have studied to
date, I have never heard of anything so degrading or
beneath humanity. Hopefully, such scenes will never
ever be witnessed in the future. Dead bodies were lying all around on the roads, on paths and everywhere.
Previously I used to be scared of seeing a dead body
but after seeing all this, there is no fear left in me.
Perhaps, I have become accustomed to this.

Trains were made to stop at the Sirhind canal, where
all Muslim passengers were killed and thrown in the
water. In the end the canal was full of dead bodies.
Then they had to shut off the canal in order to clear
it out. Thousands of dead bodies were piled up on
railway crossing gates.

At our station, no Muslims were left alive on any
train. In fact, one day two families of Muslims were
traveling in a 1st class carriage. After the train left
from the previous station Sirhind, they telephoned
Khanna station to inform about the Muslim passengers. The train was made to stop at Khanna and
everyone in that carriage was ordered to come out.
An Englishman, who was in that carriage refused and
fired with his pistol. One man on the platform got
wounded and after that, firing started from outside,
so all passengers on the train shut their windows.
One boy quickly sprinkled oil on the carriage and
set it on fire. I have no idea what the train was carrying, because it went up in flames very quickly.
Approximately 15 men got saved, the rest, including
the Englishman, got burnt inside the train. Not even

the remains of those people were found. Water was
sprinkled on the carriage to put out the fire. The
remaining carriages at the rear were left unharmed
so they were separated. The train is still standing at
Khanna. The luggage of a Sikh man from Africa who
was traveling on that train, also got burnt quite badly.

Your brother, Shangara Singh

Personal recollections of the riots in India by
Parminder, Shangara Singh's son.

*I was only five years old but I remember the terrifying fear rising
within me every time those bells rang on the roof of our house, accompanied by loud shouts "Muslims are coming". I also remember a
visit to a neighboring village with my father. We stood at the edge
of the village, with me clutching his hand tightly. I could see the
burnt down houses all around us. I noticed a small dirt covered book
lying on the ground. I picked it up and brought it home with me. At
night I would keep that book under my pillow. I still do not know
why I did that. Was it a comforting connection with the owner of
the book, perhaps a child of my age, who I could relate to? Or did I
latch on to it because the book was the only thing that made sense
to me, in the dark, terrifying world engulfing us*

From Shangara Singh, 20.11.1947, Lalheri

Dear brothers Gurmukh Singh and Kartar Singh, Sat
Siri Akal

We witnessed very horrendous incidents and situations where a dog's death caused sadness, but a

person's life had no value. Wealthy people who had never bought anything for under 4 'pai' and had always feasted on a vast variety of foods, were brought down to such a level that they even struggled to cover their bodies with clothes and were roaming around looking for a morsel of food. They were sitting lost and abandoned, along with their children, on the roadsides in the towns. People's lives have been turned upside down and their hearts are filled with terror. Even now, we have no faith in anything. We have witnessed incidents which are beneath humanity. We saw them burning women and children alive.

I will need to write a book if I start writing all the details. Suffice it to say that these incidents continued all through September and some days of October too. Atrocities were committed on both sides. If they killed four Sikhs then people from Barr killed fifteen in return. Village after village was burnt down, causing a lot of destruction. Trains were burnt and destroyed. Jathe wale [Sikh groups] were asking drivers to stop trains by raising their hands, just like you stop cars, wherever and whenever they liked, in order to climb in. On occasion, it happened that all passengers on the trains were massacred.

Until now, trains are running without tickets. All trains, including goods trains, are full inside and on the roof. Previously people used to be afraid of sitting on the roofs of trains, but now there are less people inside the trains and more on top of the roofs, for easy escape. The trains are filled to the brim, people are even squeezing into the space between coaches and also hanging on to the axles of the train. Up to 10,000 people are traveling on each train.

Muslims who survived from our area are at Ambala Camp, and are leaving for Pakistan in a day or two. There is a Muslim camp in Ludhiana, which is being guarded by soldiers of Balauch Regiment. Muslims have gathered in hundreds of thousands in camps in big cities and on the road to Amritsar. Some are going to Pakistan on foot, others on loaded trains.

Now there is a pause in killings and Muslims are coming out of hiding and going to camps. A few days ago, I learned that some of the Muslims from our village reached Malerkotla camp. In Ludhiana, a 2-mile-wide Muslim camp has been set up from Budha River to Phillaur. In these camps there is excessive garbage. Cholera is spreading fast, and many people are dying from disease and starvation.

One and a half lakh [one hundred and fifty thousand] Muslims left from Khanna. There were thousands of gaddas [bullock carts] accompanying the kafilas. Because of the long distance they had to cover, they set off at 6am and were seen walking past continuously until 7 pm.

Proper postal service has not resumed yet. I have not been able to go to Ramgarh for quite a while, because no trains stop there. I informed you previously that none of us from the entire village were able to go to the farmland during the period of 15th August to September, except to bring green fodder for the cattle. All our time and energy were spent on standing on guard, trying to save lives. We finally started to plow the farmland at the end of September.

A couple of Muslim men in hiding, came to ask for atta [flour] for roti [chappatis], which we collected and gave to them. They told us that Muslims from our village, who were camping at Ambala, have all left two days ago in two kafilas [caravan or foot column]. Our mistris [skilled builders], lohaars [blacksmiths] have all gone to Pakistan.

Your brother, Shangara Singh

From Shangara Singh, 26.11.1947, Lalheri

Dear brothers Gurmukh Singh and Kartar Singh, Sat Siri Akal

We resumed all our jobs at the end of September. We had already planted maize before the riots but it was not in our fate to even lift a khurpa [trowel] to do any digging/weeding or tend to it after planting. At first, there were no rains for a long time, but later, it rained non-stop daily, beyond limits. Very few maize plants reached a height of five feet, so the produce is not sufficient even for our own consumption. It was gathered a week ago.

More land will be plowed soon, followed by seeding. Because the mill hasn't been operating fully during these times, the cash crop that would normally be processed at the mill, is lying around in their goddams [warehouses] and is going to waste.

The rivers got flooded, even more so than previous years, due to long lasting, heavy rains. River Sutlej's bridge collapsed and a part of the railway line got swept away by water currents. Only one line is functional now. At a camp of Muslims which was right on the riverside, thousands of people and their belongings got swept away and got lost in the floods. Even GT Road, from Ludhiana to River Sutlej was broken by the floods. Various small bridges between Sutlej and Beas rivers were also damaged.

Stray cattle [left behind by Muslim refugees going over to Pakistan] are wandering around, eating a lot of the crops on our farms. We had to remove them four times from our farmland near the road.

At first, we had three bulls at home, plus Gurdial Singh's calf that was born this year. We caught one stray bull that was wandering around, two days ago. So, now we have two pairs of bulls. In our village, approximately fifty stray bulls, buffaloes and camels were wandering around, which are now registered with the Government. It is the same in all villages. The Government is assessing the needs and redistributing these among villagers and refugees from Barr. It was our turn to have the bull officially allocated to us, but for some reason, our turn got passed. So, the stray bull will stay with us, for now.

The Government is carrying out searches for the stuff people have looted from Muslims' houses, and is taking it away. Muslims couldn't carry away wheat etc. with them, so hundreds of maunds were left lying in deserted homes. There is a lot of anxiety in the heart now, about planting wheat as there is no-one to sell it to. In our village, wheat and other belongings from 4-5 muslim houses have been taken to a dharamsala [a sanctuary, a rest house for travelers].

The children are all well but they are very frightened. Nanhi and Lakha's [his sons] school is now closed. It was due to open on 29/10, but now it will open on 29/11, if there are no disturbances.

Now there is a need for another Gurudwara so three adjacent, vacant Muslim houses, Rehmat Lambardar's haveli [large house] on his farmland, along with Gufoor and Naksh's houses have been designated as Gurudwara land. All three houses are now enclosed within four boundary walls. They have repaired the large house and converted it into a temple building. The Sikh religious flag Nishan Sahib is on a pole outside and the Sikh holy book has been set up in the main hall of the house. They have performed akhand paath-bhog [Sikh prayers] to bless the building as a Sikh Gurudwara.

Brothers Naksh and Gufoor's [Muslim brothers] houses are being used for travelers needing shelter, especially for Sikh refugees who are arriving from Pakistan daily, at the local train station. Hot meals are served there.

The village Gurudwara is making progress now and there is a lot of activity in the evenings. Girls are being taught to read and write in Punjabi. Boys can also attend classes one day a week.

At present, Miya Singh [a converted Sikh] stays in a small house next to the Gurudwara. He is there all the time and works for both communities. Miya Singh will bring other converted men here, to make good use of the house. Quite a few boys have taken Amrit [converted to Sikhism] and a room has been prepared for them to live in. Chani's (Kartar's second son] shepherd friend Kheru has become a Singh and he now lives at the Gurudwara.

The refugees from Pakistan are being housed in schools, so they are all closed until 1st March. Only schools up to Class 4 are open. Khanna's big school has 800 military men in it, for protection because Khanna's name is at the top for surveillance after the train derailment. They will try to free the Muslim women that have been captured.

Now we have a new problem, the war has started in Kashmir. There is even greater fear in people's hearts, which is causing lots of disturbances. If the situation gets any worse, then we might have to go also. I do not know of other places but in Khanna some people have assembled to cause disturbances.

Yusuf's complete clan and all Muslim skilled workers have left from our village and have reached Pakistan. Now people from Barr [refugees from Pakistan] have taken their place, and have started planting on their land.

On Dusherra festival, an effigy of Ravan was burnt but fireworks were prohibited. Curfew was imposed on Diwali day. It was not celebrated, due to so many homeless and distressed people wandering about.

Your brother, Shangara Singh

From Shangara Singh, 24.12.1947, Lalheri

Dear brothers Gurmukh Singh and Kartar Singh, Sat Siri Akal

As mentioned previously, the rains this year have fallen like never before and our "Bakshiwala" animal outhouse was totally destroyed. This has put us in even more difficulties, on top of the existing ones. To get the outhouse back to its original condition, lintels and beams will need to be replaced, as the roof has caved in, and walls have collapsed.

In the end I am compelled to write to you for help, as a debt of Rs 235 has accumulated with Gurdial Singh shopkeeper. We buy everything like daal [lentils] etc. on credit from him. Now with the added problem of rain damage, I am under great pressure and do not know who to turn to. The crops are not flourishing, there is debt on my head and I need to repair the house. Cold weather is approaching, which will make it difficult to fix the house, and I cannot get bricks. I am now awaiting your advice and instructions.

We are very happy to hear that Kartar Singh has been promoted to a Guard, which will make his work easier and also the wages will increase quite a bit.

I wrote to you that Bebeji wants to see a photo of all the kids. In her heart she believes that she is not going to stay alive now, although we have not said anything to her about her illness. So, send us a photo of all the children. If possible, I will also try to get a photo taken of Bebeji, which can be enlarged afterwards. It is very cold over here now. Bebeji's health always gets worse in cold weather. She has really slowed down and has been getting a fever for a month so we called a doctor and she is a bit better with medication. Bebeji is losing heart now, and keeps crying.

Your brother Shangara Singh

Impact of India's Partition on Indians in Kenya

From Kartar's daughter, Perminder

I was ten years old when India got independence on August 15, 1947. Partition of the country into India and Pakistan caused a lot of bitterness amongst some people in Kenya though most people did not let it affect their relations with each other. In 1947, news spread very slowly due to lack of telephones, radios, televisions or internet which helped to prevent the violent and bloody conflict of the Indian subcontinent from spilling into Kenya. Until then the French Revolution was considered the bloodiest but the Partition of India was even worse.

I remember 2 incidents:

We had a corner house in Ngara railway quarters at that time and somebody wrote a slogan on our wall at night, saying "Pakistan Murdabad" [death to Pakistan]. Our dad Kartar Singh saw it in the morning and I remember that he quickly washed it off with the help of my brother Biri (Balbir Singh) and our domestic help, in order to diffuse rising tensions between Sikhs/Hindus and Muslims.

On Independence Day, our dad took Biri and me to join a big procession that passed through Desai Road, Nairobi. We walked to Desai Memorial Hall, where some speeches were given. We continued to celebrate India's Independence Day for a few years, by decorating our front yards with lights and Indian flags.

CHAPTER 6

1948
Death of a Beloved Mother

Kartar and his siblings loved, respected and worshiped their mother Be-beji. Reading about the family's struggles, one wonders if Kartar's elder and younger brother felt that returning to India in 1941 was a big mistake, but tough as it was, it turned out to be a blessing in disguise for Bebeji. She got the opportunity to spend the final years of her life surrounded by her beloved sons and their families. She adored her grandchildren and treasured every moment spent with them.

Above all, destiny played its hand by keeping Kartar's younger brother Shangara, a most selfless soul, by her side during the sunset of her life. His love and devotion helped to make her final days comfortable. He always put her needs at the forefront and carried her around on his shoulders when she was unable to walk towards the end. Their sister Kartar Kaur frequently came from Ramgarh to assist him in taking care of their mother in her final days.

The brothers gave their mother a send-off befitting a Goddess, as that is exactly what she was in their eyes and heart.

The letters written in 1948 reached a peak in personal and financial challenges, in the aftermath of partition.

From Shangara Singh, 4.5.1948, Lalheri

Brothers Gurmukh Singh Ji & Kartar Singh Ji, Sat Siri Akal.

It is good that you [Gurmukh Singh] have been transferred to Kisumu. Firstly, it is like Punjab because
everything is easily available there and secondly,
Kisumu's air might suit Gurbachan Kaur better, to
enable her health to improve.

What can I write? I am finding it difficult to write
these ill-fated words with my own hand. Bebeji's condition has finally reached an extreme state. Now it
is necessary for one person to sit by her side all the
time. She doesn't want me to be away from her, and
it is understandable. The bageecha [blossoming gar-
den] of our home is wilting and appears to be a guest
for a few days only. If she continues to live, that will
be good, but we are losing faith now. On seeing her
deteriorating condition, we took her to Ludhiana with
great difficulty to have her photograph taken. This
photo that I am sending to you, might be our very
last memory of her. You can get it enlarged or keep
it as it is. I only got three copies made, out of which
I am sending two to you [unfortunately there is no
trace of that photo - perhaps the brothers found it
too painful to see her looking so frail].

You have asked about the house; its condition is very
bad. The repair of the roof is beyond my capability, so
it has remained as such although I have been fixing
and repairing as much as I was able to. The outside
mud house has collapsed, making my problems even
worse. We need to make some arrangements to fix
the house soon.

It is very hot here. I carry Bebeji daily to the baitak
[living room, separate from the main house] which

has been thoroughly cleaned. We sprinkle water in the baitak so that a cool breeze flows through, and we sit there with her all day long, before bringing her back home at night.

Your loving brother, Shangara Singh

From Gurmukh Singh, 22.5.1948, Kisumu

Dear brother Kartar Singh Ji, Sat Siri Akal.

Although I believe you must have received the wire but, if for any reason, there has been a delay, I am writing this letter to you. I received this wire around 5 o'clock today evening:

Mother died 21st

So, what can I write to you about the emotions that are rising within my heart. The common link in the chain of our home [family] has broken today and now everyone is the master of their own will. The deep sadness about this is that although she was going to die one day, and even though she had spent a good lifetime, we don't know for which sin of hers she had to bear this punishment of having to tolerate so much lingering pain and suffering before she gave up her life.

At the moment, my heart is not feeling right and my brain is not functioning, so I am at a loss as to what to write. The only thing that is necessary to mention now is that you discuss with Bibi Karam Kaur [their elder sister in Nairobi] as to what needs to be done, and send a letter to them at home, accordingly. Write within a day or two so that they receive our letters before they hold Barah [ceremony performed twelve days after death]. We need to arrange to send some money. You wrote to me about sending some shillings. I will try to send the remaining 200-300 shillings, whatever I can manage, if not sooner, then definitely after getting my wages, so that it reaches there before Barah. I have also written to Shangara Singh that Kartar Singh will send him full instructions after discussing with Bibiji Karam Kaur.

My heart feels very restless and uneasy today.

As always, your brother Gurmukh Singh

From Shangara Singh, 16.6.1948, Lalheri

Janab brothers Gurmukh Singh Ji & Kartar Singh Ji, Sat Siri Akal.

I received your letters dated 18/5 and 22/5. I have also received all 3 letters from Kartar Singh. Rs 99 and Rs 200, were both received before the Barah ceremony. Kartar Singh's letter containing a draft for Rs 330 was received today.

Today everything is over regarding Bebeji, and until now having people around, and the activity of Maharaj's Prakash [prayers] kept me from thinking of her. Now the house appears very empty without her. She has taken the raunuk [hustle bustle] of our home away with her. I miss her all the time and see her before my eyes, sitting on a charpai [bed], fanning herself with a hand-held fan, just like she used to. As soon as I enter the house, I automatically call out to Bebeji, from habit. I don't know whether this will always continue to be so. We are all crying separately, hiding our tears from each other. There is no-one here to console us or give us support.

Bebeji really suffered during the last month so considering that, we feel what has happened is good. But still the heart wanted her to remain sitting near us, like always. Just seeing her sitting on her charpai gave me a lot of support. Whenever a problem cropped up, I would sit and discuss it with her before taking any action. I used to lighten the burden on my heart by talking to her. Now the pain in my heart is eating away at me. I miss her so much. That is why we have kept Bibi Kartar Kaur [their younger sister] here at Lalheri, to be with us for some days. Without a doubt, I put all my efforts into doing Bebeji's seva [taking care of her]. I made sure that she would not feel any discomfort of any kind. Whatever Bebeji asked for, was always given to her. All the time, two of us continued to sit with her. We gave her a bath daily and changed her clothes. Two days before her death Bebeji requested to have a muslin kameez [shirt] stitched for her as she felt too warm at night. We put the muslin shirt on her on Wednesday but she had only two days left to wear it. It was removed on Friday evening. People from our village and all around are full of praise and are saying "This is the way to take care of a Maa when she needs looking after." Even when I was carrying her around on my shoulders, I never felt or thought of that as any kind of trouble. In fact, taking care of her made my heart feel happy.

A week before her death, Lakha [Shangara's younger son] got very ill and his condition was very serious. We kept him downstairs while Bebeji was in the chobara [the room on the rooftop] but she kept crying and saying that she didn't want a tragic wound inflicted on her heart during her final days. On her insistence, we had to take Lakha's charpai (bed) upstairs so she could be near him. She has taken away with her all the thoughts that she had kept hidden in her heart. Perhaps I wrote to you that Bebeji asked me to write and request Bibi Karam Kaur [their elder sister in Nairobi] to send her a white 'chicken di chaddar' [dupatta, headscarf made of special embroidered cotton] if someone is coming here [from Africa], as hers was worn out. Now my heart cries whenever I remember this. She kept telling me to ask Bibi Karam Kaur to come and see her for just one day, even if she needs to return home the very next day. I find it hard to compose a letter when my thoughts are full of her. I miss her so much. Like me, Wazir Singh keeps crying and has become ill. He hasn't eaten food for several days and has lost weight and grown thin and weak. I have tried hard to make him understand but he just keeps saying "I don't know what has happened."

Secondly, this cycle of adversity that is surrounding me from all four directions, has created even more problems. Four days after Bebeji's death, our camel also departed from this world. Our hearts had not recovered from our loss, when this burden descended on us. I don't know why Waheguru keeps piling on all the troubles of the world on our heads, but I still have full faith in him. If he wishes us to spend better days, then he will remove this ongoing cycle of troubles and will look at us with benevolence.

Bebeji's cremation took place on 22nd May [the day after she died]. We placed a reshmi dupatta [silk cloth] on the palki [palanquin- a type of platform to transport the dead], and decorated it with bunting.

ACCORDING TO TRADITION, ONLY MALE MEMBERS CARRIED THE BODY ON ITS FINAL JOURNEY TO CREMATION GROUND. SHANGARA AND HIS YOUNGER BROTHER GURDIAL WITH BEBEJI'S GRANDSONS, BIDDING THEIR FINAL FAREWELL TO BEBEJI.

Villagers scattered flowers as we carried the palki. At the Gurudwara, Atma Ram played the harmonium while religious hymns were recited. We carried the palki from the Gurudwara to the cremation grounds.

Villagers joined us along the way, as we walked. It all went well and her cremation was done with full honors, although at the time tears were flowing like raindrops from my eyes. Afterwards, Gurdial [the youngest brother] and I both took the ashes and scattered them in Ganga [River Ganges]. That was Bebeji's last ishnaan [bath] in the holy water.

On our return from Ganga, we started Maharaj ka Prakash [reading of Guru Granth Sahib, the holy book]. The bhog of Akhand Path [completion of prayers] and Barah ceremony were held on Sunday 6th June.

We served sweet rice to villagers. All our relatives were served a meal at our home. We cooked the food ourselves and served them homemade laddoos [Indian sweets]. This was followed by the Barah ceremony from 12.30-2.00 pm.

Two utensils were given to Kirpal and two to Pritamo's daughter. We gave bedding consisting of an Indian quilt, sheet, and pillow plus Rs 5 in lieu of a charpai [bed] to Pritamo's daughter. For jewelry, we gifted her a gold chain made of five circular beads and stones which cost us Rs 40. We also gave her a lady's suit & dupatta [head scarf] in the memory of Walid Sahib (our late father). These clothes were of good quality and were displayed to the panchayat [village govern-ing body]. Some lesser quality clothes were given to a couple of other people. Approximately Rs 30 were spent on cash payments to pay bahadurs [workers, helpers, hymn reciters etc.]. I have not kept an item-ized breakdown of these payments.

[The authors were unable to establish the family connection to Pritamo's daughter or Kirpal. According to tradition, such gifts were given to girls in the husband's family. Since Bebeji's late husband Sham was an only child, the recipients of the gifts were probably the offspring of a relative whom Sham treated as a sister].

The bhog [completion of prayers] ceremony was performed from 2-4 pm. For us Bebeji was a Goddess, for us she was our father, for us she was the most important person in the village. Keeping our love and respect for our mother at the forefront, the Granthi [priest] gave a nice speech and spoke very highly of our Bebeji and her life. Four items of clothing were given to him.

Afterwards, the pagri [turban] ceremony started. A turban was given by each of our relatives.

Now day by day, memories of Bebeji are engulfing me. My heart cries at all little reminders of her. I thought I might be able to forget her loss, but now I believe that my heart will never be free of thoughts of her. Bebeji took away the worries of several matters locked within her heart. Oh well, may Waheguru give peace to her soul. The children also miss Bebeji a lot. What can I write? Whenever I think of her, tears start flowing from my eyes, making it difficult to write this letter. We will feel the darkness even more after Bibi Kartar Kaur [the younger sister] returns to Ramgarh in two to four days.

I followed your instructions, and did whatever you asked me to do. I don't think I have exceeded. I had never seen an occasion like this before and had no experience of what happens at such times. I really had to harden my heart to fulfill my responsibilities and to carry out these arrangements to the best of my ability. Waheguru made me face all this. I am sending a photo of Bebeji's cremation to you. The boy who took the photo didn't know how to adjust the correct time in the very bright sunshine and gave it too much time (exposure). Anyway, this is the final memory of her.

Dharam Singh and Gunaiya got married by paying Rs 2500 for the two wives.

Amar Singh (of Lalheri) got married to a refugee Muslim girl in Ludhiana, by paying Rs 1500 cash for her. He is separated from his first wife and this marriage was done in secrecy a month and a half ago.

As always, your brother Shangara Singh

Shangara expressed the depth of his feelings beautifully. Perhaps, ending his intense and poignant letters on a lighter note, by narrating an interesting anecdote about some village gossip or scandal, was his way of lessening the impact of the painful letters on his brothers.

Note from Kartar's daughter Pinder:

Amar Singh's children had Sikh names. His wife was kind and welcoming, and always offered cold lassi to my brother, my cousins and myself when we stayed in our village Lalheri for a short while for my wedding, in June1963.

From Shangara Singh, 18.9.1948, Lalheri

Brothers Gurmukh Singh & Kartar Singh, Sat Siri Akal,

After completing all ceremonies for Bebeji, I owed Rs 550. But then the camel died, and calamity descended on my life. To buy another camel was very costly and I was not able to borrow such a high sum from anywhere in the village. But not buying one meant an end to the farm work. In the end, after trying very hard, I borrowed Rs 400 from Dass Bajaj, who did me a big favor by not charging any interest on it. A money lender would have charged me another Rs 50-60 as interest. I got together the remaining sum from here and there and bought a camel for Rs 630. But I had to sell our buffalo for Rs 370, in order to raise enough money to pay back the loan. Now I have returned the money that I borrowed. The buf-falo was due to give birth in about 20 days but I had to sell it out of necessity. If Waheguru [God] desires, we will see about the milk. Oxen and the new camel are all well. None of this is in anyone's control, it is just my bad luck.

We have collected money for morabba-bandhi [land consolidation where small pieces of land owned by farmers were joined together in one plot to make farms more productive, after independence/parti-tion]. The rupees were sent to Ambala Head Office, but so far nothing has been done. Perhaps, it will get done once the land has been allocated to refugees, but you never know.

A month ago, Rehmat Lohaar [blacksmith] came back. Slowly, other Muslims keep arriving. Hopefully they will soon be allocated a house by the Government.

Gurudwara's condition is good and it is running well with lots of activity. A water pump has been installed and lots of flowers have been planted in the garden. In the school approximately fifteen boys and girls learn Punjabi, and the new Granthi [priest] who is well educated, teaches Maths too. Quite a few girls are studying there.

Love to kids.

As always, your loving brother Shangara Singh

CHAPTER 7

1949
Departure of Third Brother
for Kenya

When Shangara decided to return to India in 1941, little did he realize that due to circumstances beyond his control, he would be stuck there for the most challenging eight years of his life. At first, he kept himself occupied with his employment at Simla and later by helping on the farm in between temporary jobs, but after his elder brother Gurmukh left for Kenya in January 1945, Shangara was suddenly left in charge of a rapidly sinking ship. The financial problems created by the Second World War, which had continued to get worse each year due to long term unemployment, high inflation, rationing and restrictions on entry to Kenya, reached a climax after India's partition on August 15, 1947.

They say that people who experienced the soul-destroying atrocities of partition between India and Pakistan were so traumatized that they could never bring themselves to talk about it afterwards. From Shangara's letters, it appears that he too temporarily suffered from post-traumatic stress after personally experiencing and witnessing the harrowing violence during the gruesome period of partition. Inability to tend to the farm during partition, followed by droughts and heavy rainfall led to poor harvests. He was certainly under a lot of stress with partition, Bebeji's illness followed by her death, shortage of money, debt problems, unemployment, domestic animals dying, and flood damage to the house.

While reading his letters, one feels compelled to pray for the expedition of his departure to Kenya. One can only imagine the insurmountable sense of freedom and relief he must have felt on leaving behind the horrors of the two years 1947-1949.

For Shangara's work permit, Kartar obtained a letter of job offer from his brother-in-law Hukam's cousin who owned the Central Garage in downtown Nairobi. The job offer was for a car mechanic. Having a British passport on which he had previously traveled to Kenya in 1937 and having worked in Kenya as an electrician [which was on the special skills list] helped to strengthen Shangara's case.

As in the case of Gurmukh, by showing the job offer letter, Kartar was able to get "Special Endorsement Certificate" by paying a deposit of 685 shillings, to be refunded after one year of useful employment as an immigrant in Kenya.

On arrival in Bombay to obtain tickets for his family Shangara was confronted with two new requirements. It is not clear from the letters if these bureaucratic hurdles were to extract bribes from desperate travelers.

1. The payment of the deposit had to be stamped on the Endorsement Certificate. Shangara got around it by paying an extra Rs 215 for a guarantee bond, from the money he received at the last minute, via wire transfer of Rs 250 by his brother-in-law Hukam Singh

2. The letter of a job offer had to be accompanied by a form filled by a potential employer. Shangara resolved this by authorizing the travel agent to fill one out.

The letters of 1949 depict the last-minute struggles to resolve bureaucratic hurdles caused by changing immigration laws during the era when communications were at a snail's pace.

From Shangara Singh, 31.1.1949, Lalheri

Dear brothers Gurmukh Singh and Kartar Singh Ji,
Sat Siri Akal.

I received your two letters but couldn't reply earlier because it was difficult to write with my right hand which got injured during construction of the wall of the house. I hope you will forgive me for the delay.

I have received Kartar Singh's letter along with the permit for Kenya and Rs 300. A few days ago, I also received your (Gurmukh Singh's) Rs 100. I want to let you know that I had no other option but to use the money sent by you two, to pay the builders working on the house.

All paperwork for my passport is ready, the only delay now is Jaswant Kaur's permit. I will submit the application for both passports on the day I receive her permit. The fee for a passport has now gone up from Rs 6 to Rs 10. I need your advice regarding booking of our tickets. Do I need to write to Lal Devi or the MM office? Also, do I have to send the fare first or can I pay it before departure? I will start making preparations as soon as the passports are ready.

Reflecting back, one can say I came to India of my own free will, but I did not have any choice about returning to Kenya earlier. I am glad I came and was here to comfort our mother in the final days of her life. Our Bebeji, who faced great difficulties all her life for our sake. Me writing all this with my own hand does not look good on me, but it frightens me to think of what the situation would have been if I had not been here. Just thinking about it makes my heart well up with emotion. The last days of her life were terrible and I felt so helpless despite being here.

I have never spoken about the shock I felt after her death. When I think about it my heart and eyes cry. Even now I cannot be in the house on my own. Jaswant Kaur [his wife] and the kids had gone to her village Rattanheri to attend a prayer ceremony, but I had to go and fetch Nanhi and Lakha [his sons] because I dreaded being on my own at night. There is no knowing of my life, but we will talk when we are together. To keep Bebeji's memory alive forever, I am making a small memorial, a small token to remember her by. I have constructed six feet long and 2 feet wide Chontra type platform, on top of which I have built a memorial of bricks and stones. I will make a place to put a lamp on it and will also write Bebeji's date of death.

Our animal house is now ready, the doors and windows have been fitted. In the last few days, we have started to keep our cattle there. To avoid flooding, the floor has been raised to a level higher than the lane, by forming a base layer of hardcore. Lintels have been placed at a height of 10 feet. Two windows have been built on either side of the door, and another two are at the back.

All this work was accomplished with great difficulty. I had to borrow Rs 125 on top of Rs 400 sent by you two. The original estimate was low as it would have taken less days in the long daylight hours of summer. I had to pay Rs 40 extra on labor, due to shorter winter days.

Bhima has got himself a 25-year-old woman for Rs 1400. He got her through Haria. Following a police officer's visit to their house, I came to know that she is not from the surrounding area.

Now Bebeji's love has been removed from letters, something she used to ask me to write repeatedly.

Your loving brother Shangara Singh, Lalheri.

From Shangara Singh, 11.2.1949, Lalheri

Dear Brothers Gurmukh Singh, Kartar Singh Ji, Sat Siri Akal.

I received Kartar Singh's letter which contained Jaswant Kaur's permit.

I heard there was communal violence in Durban, South Africa, similar to what happened in Punjab, which sounds quite worrying and frightening. Recently there was also a rumor that Africans in Kenya have started boycotting Indian businesses but I could not find the details.

I sent off all the forms after receiving the permit. I am trying to come as soon as possible. Whatever Waheguru wishes will happen. Who would remember him if everything keeps happening according to one's wishes?

For some time now we have not had any milk as our buffalo at home had to be sold. The cow is not expected to give birth for at least another month and a half [to start producing milk for her expected offspring]. After a lot of consideration, I bought one buffalo, so that the children would get to drink milk. But due to our bad luck, that buffalo has been lying sick for the last 15 days and she cannot even fulfill the needs of the calf. We took her to Khanna hospital several times and the Rattanheri veterinarian doctor tried lots of medicines and traditional cures, but her condition remains bad. She does not eat or drink anything at all. It seems the whole household's milk has gone away with Bebeji. Since the day Bebeji passed away let alone milk, not even tea is in our destiny. This is the story of our situation, what more can I write.

Children are well and my intention is to leave in the month of May after their exams, but that depends on the passports. The rest is as you suggest.

As always, your brother Shangara Singh.

From Shangara Singh, 24.3.1949, Lalheri

Dear brother Kartar Singh Ji, Sat Siri Akal,

I have received Jaswant Kaur's passport but my paperwork was returned because of the fighting with Pakistan, and has now been resubmitted [perhaps due to Shangara's birth place being in Pakistan?]. Due to the children's education, we will have to delay our departure to May, soon after their exams. Leaving before exams will waste a whole year of their schooling as they will have to repeat a year in Africa. For our preparation, I will need to get 2 sets of clothes stitched for each one of us. You have a better idea of how much money I need for traveling and for the ship's fares. After receiving your rupees, if there is any left over from the fares then I will buy a few other things that will be needed.

This year has started very badly for us. Bebeji has taken the blossom of this house with her. First, she passed away, then the camel died, and then all that building work needed to be done. Now, the buffalo which was worth Rs 300-400 has died. You brothers have met our needs to a great extent but you were not able to meet all of them. I am very thankful to you both. I will bring the dharis [cotton homespun rugs] and khes [traditional blankets] with me. If you need anything else, write by return mail.

As always, your loving brother Shangara Singh.

From Shangara Singh, 29.3.1949, Lalheri

Dear brother Kartar Singh Ji, Sat Siri Akal.

I have not yet received your money order of 760 shillings. Perhaps there was a delay somewhere, and it will arrive soon.

I am very grateful to you for getting me out of this adversity. Rs 500 will cover travel fares, Rs 350 for the ship's tickets, Rs 100 for train fare to Bombay, and the remaining Rs 50 on train tickets from Mombasa to Nairobi.

I do not have the full understanding but you know about the costs incurred in the preparation for departure, like clothes, shoes, cooking utensils, ration for the ship journey plus the expenditure of our stay in Bombay. I can come over quickly once all of this has been organized. I am still waiting for my passport to arrive. I wrote to Lal Devi a week ago to send me the ships' sailing list so I can finalize everything. Reading what you wrote about coming over makes my heart beat faster in anticipation. One part of me wants to leave right this moment but the other part feels nervous about leaving.

I received Gurmukh Singh's letter at the same time as yours, and will answer it separately. Sat Siri Akal from all of us to all of you and love to the children.

Your brother Shangara Singh.

From Shangara Singh, 2.5.49, Lalheri

Dear brothers Gurmukh Singh, Kartar Singh Ji, Sat Siri Akal.

I have not yet received the money order which you sent but hopefully it will arrive soon.

I have finally received my passport, after writing two letters to Simla. Lal Devi from Bombay wrote to say that the first ship leaves on 11th May, but for that the time is very short. The second ship leaves on 1st June, which suits us so I have sent the money for our fares to MM office today. If we get a place then we will leave from here around 28th May. I decided against booking through Lal Devi in order to save the commission they charge. I have not yet received the typed letter that you said you would send, so remember to send it soon.

Kashmira Singh (brother-in-law Hukam Singh's brother) is coming with me and I am coming as soon as possible.

As always, your loving brother Shangara Singh, Lalheri.

From Shangara Singh, 23.5.1949, Lalheri

Dear Brother Kartar Singh Ji, Sat Siri Akal.

I sent our fares to Bombay on 1st May, the day I received my passport, and was waiting for their reply, which I have now received:

"In confirmation having regretted your name and names of your family for deck accommodations from Bombay to Mombasa. We shall advise you as soon as we are able to offer you accommodation."

Today I am writing to Mackinnon Mackenzie again to give me a place on the first ship leaving. When we went to Ludhiana for inoculations, we met a friend from Kenya, who told me that the first ship is leaving on 8ᵗʰ June. It will be good if we get a place on that one.

All the harvest has been lifted, and people's accounts have been settled. This was the main weight on my mind. The account with some people was quite high but if I had ignored it and just left, that would have brought disgrace to us. Now I have dealt with everything, all preparations are complete and I am ready to leave.

We had a prayer ceremony on the day of Bebeji's anniversary.

Sat Siri Akal from us to all of you. Love to the children.

Your loving brother Shangara Singh, Lalheri.

From Shangara Singh, 1.6.1949, Lalheri

Dear brothers Gurmukh Singh, Kartar Singh Ji, Sat Siri Akal. Here all the family is well and we ask Waheguru for your families' wellbeing.

The news is that Gurmukh Singh's letter and the Rs 225 sent by you were received 3-4 days ago so there is no shortage of rupees in any way. All my preparations are complete and money for fares has been sent. After learning that a ship was departing on 8ᵗʰ June, I wrote again to Mackenzie to give me a definite place on that ship. The sad thing is that their reply, which I am sending to you, is troubling me a lot. They say that they cannot give me a place on any ship during the month of June, I must be ready and await my turn.

As ever your loving brother Shangara Singh.

British India Steam Navigation Co., Ltd.

(INCORPORATED IN ENGLAND.)

THE REPLY TO BE ADDRESSED
MACKINNON MACKENZIE & CO.,
AGENTS.
BOMBAY.

IN REPLY PLEASE QUOTE
No. P/B.I.
(No. 1)

Bombay, 28th May, 194 9.

POST BOX No. 122.

Telegraphic Address: " MACKINNONS "
Telephone : 25021.

Shangara Singh, Esq.,
C/o Atma Ram Bhagwan Dass,
Cloth Merchants, Khanna,
Ludhiana.

Dear Sir,

We are in receipt of your letter dated the 23rd May and in reply we regret we are unable to offer you accommodation in any of the steamers sailing in June 1949.

You will therefore have to await for your turn.

We confirm having received your Money Order for Rs.454/8/-.

Yours faithfully,
Pro MACKINNON MACKENZIE & CO.,

Agents.

BMasc/

From Shangara Singh, 8.7.1949, Bombay

Dear Brother Kartar Singh Ji, Sat Siri Akal.

As of today, the morning of 8ᵗʰ July, I have not yet received any reply to the wires.

All of us including Kashmira Singh reached Bombay and are staying here at Lal Devi's. I received a letter from the office saying "You report on 6ᵗʰ July and the ship will leave on 8ᵗʰ July." But the departure has been delayed to 12ᵗʰ July, which may work in our favor.

First of all, there is no indication of a bond on the permit which you sent, although I have seen it entered on other permits. If you had found out all this beforehand or made arrangements for it over there, then I would have been spared this stress and tussle over here today, when I do not have that much money. The difficulties are much more now compared to the time when I came to Africa for the first time with you. I do not understand why only struggle is fated for me, in getting to Africa.

Secondly the main reason which is giving me a lot of bother about the permit is that the Central Garage authority letter should have been sent to me first. On receipt of which, an agreement form would have been completed and sent to the Immigrant Office. Only then, they would have given me the 'No Objection Certificate', on receipt of which the ship's tickets would have been issued. Now I feel helpless in all these aspects and cannot understand what is to be done. Lal Devi's son suggested that you should send a wire from Kenya to the Permit people so that they can inform the Immigrant Office that Lal Devi can fill in the agreement form on behalf of Central Garage.

So yesterday I sent an ordinary wire to Hukam Singh Ji to request this and also to ask for rupees for the bond. I didn't send an express wire in order to save money, as that would have cost me Rs 40. The only reason for sending the wire to Hukam Singh was that he would get it quicker as you might have been away on duty.

If the wire and the rupees are received in time then we will catch this ship. Otherwise, there is no thakana [place to go to]. Lal Devi will charge us additional rent for the dates 6th to 12th. A quarter fare has been charged for the little Guddi [Khushdev] also, who is under 3 years old, as this additional fare became effective from 28/4. One problem follows another. We can't go back home and I am not in a position to stay here until the next ship which leaves on 4/8, as there are many expenses with the children. The rent alone over here is Rs 200. I will inform you if we are unable to travel on this ship.

Now I am waiting for Hukam Singh's wire. You must definitely come to Mombasa on our arrival and if there is any other formality to be completed, then get it done beforehand. I have no knowledge of all this. If I am left behind then whatever Waheguru wishes, will happen. Kashmira Singh has got his ticket so he will definitely be coming

From us, Sat Siri Akal and love to the children.

From Shangara Singh to Gurmukh Singh, 11/7/49, Bombay

Dear brother Gurmukh Singh Ji

I had a lot of trouble dealing with all the complex formalities required these days. Finally, Lal Devi filled the agreement form on behalf of Central Garage and submitted it today. I have just returned with the tickets. It was all very stressful but with the grace of Waheguru, everything was completed in time. Hopefully, if Waheguru keeps us well, then we will meet soon. Today I have been in this place for 6 days. Here accommodation was found with great difficulty as there was a lot of rush of travelers.

You must write to Kartar Singh that he should definitely come to Mombasa when the ship docks, to assist with organizing the luggage. Also, there may be a bond or other formalities to complete, and I do not want to face any more stress. Will talk more when we meet. Also tell Jagdev Singh that his father Kashmira Singh is coming with us.

Sat Siri Akal from us to you, Gurbachan Kaur. Love to Guddi, Surmukh Singh, Maate, Ghoge.

As ever your loving brother Shangara Singh

Bombay

Our Cherished Mother, Angrez

Kartar and Angrez were blessed with eight children, six boys and two girls, during their 63 years of marriage. Together, they created a home which was full of warmth, where friends, relatives and visitors were always welcomed with open arms.

Kartar brought magic and adventure into the lives of his children and taught them to fly high, whereas Angrez, with her very practical approach to life, kept them firmly grounded to their roots. She guided them on to the right path in life, by giving them emotional, physical and spiritual strength.

Angrez was gentle, caring, selfless and considerate, always putting others before her. Bringing up eight energetic children was hard work, but she brought them up with excellent parenting skills, through her ability to remain calm, patient and empathetic at all times. She dedicated her life to her children, and like Kartar's mother Bebeji, Angrez was loved and respected like a goddess by her chidren.

Education was denied to Angrez, so she appreciated its value and encouraged her children to progress further in their endeavors. She was very intelligent and took an active interest in the subjects her children studied. She gathered a lot of knowledge by listening to their discussions during mealtimes. She was familiar with the names of Shakespeare, Napolean, Nelson, Churchill, Gandhi and Nehru.

She had great faith in God and Kartar always joked that she had a direct line to God. She was the steady rock of the family and proved to be a pillar of strength during family traumas. The tragic death of their 20-year-old son

Balbir Singh in 1954, broke their hearts, the pain of which they kept locked in their hearts, until their final days.

Epilogue

Wazir Singh, the adopted brother.

After the departure of the three brothers for Africa, Wazir continued to live in the ancestral family home, with their youngest brother Gurdial. He spent most of his time on the farm, looking after it and helping with plowing, seeding and harvesting of the crops. The farm gave him a purpose in life, a sense of belonging and the crops thrived under his loving, toiling hands. He never got married. He had no friends outside the family, and treated the farm animals as if they were his own offspring. He took his last breath on the family farm on May 28, 1965. He was changing the wheel on a gadda [oxen cart] when the cart fell on him and killed him on the spot. He was 61 years old.

Karam Kaur Mangat, eldest sister.

After migrating to Kenya in 1925, Karam lived in Kibos, near Kisumu. Kibos was the only area in Kenya where Indians were allowed to own commercial farms. She lived on a farm owned by her husband and his brothers, while her husband worked at a bank in Nairobi. All of her four children were born in Kisumu. The family moved to Nairobi in the 1940s. After renting for a few years, they finally settled in their own house in the Pangani area of Nairobi, in the late 1940s. Karam died of stomach cancer in Aga Khan Hospital in Nairobi on October 8, 1961, at the age of 55. Her husband Hukam Singh continued to live in Pangani with his family and moved back to India in the 1970s, to live with his elder son, who ran his own private hospital in Jalandhar. Hukam died in Jalandhar in 1998. He was 96.

Gurmukh Singh Sumal, elder brother.

After returning to Kenya in 1947, Gurmukh worked for the East African Railways until his retirement in late 1962. He moved with his family to India in early 1963 where he had a modern farm house constructed on the family land. In the early 1970s, after all of his four children had settled in the States, he bought a house in Chandigarh, to be near his brothers Kartar and Shangara. The three brothers were once again in the same city and enjoyed each other's company, until Gurmukh and his wife migrated to San Diego, USA in the 1990s to live with their son. Gurmukh died on December 8, 2001, at the age of 93. His wife Gurbachan spent her final years with their daughter in Los Angeles and passed away on August 26, 2014.

Kartar Kaur Mangat, elder sister

Her husband's four elder brothers had migrated to East Africa in the 1920s and 30s. Kartar and her husband Sucha stayed behind to work on the family land in Ramgarh, India. Sucha was a hard-working farmer, and spent his day working on the farm from dawn to dusk. Kartar, as a farmer's wife, was always fully occupied with her busy schedule of feeding and milking the animals and helping to prepare meals for the family and farming hands. They spent their entire lives in Ramgarh, where Sucha died on August 19, 1974. Kartar continued to live in the Ramgarh family home with her son and his family, until her death on July 1, 2000. She was 89 years old.

Kartar Singh Sumal

After retiring from his Railways job in Kenya on September 30, 1962, Kartar returned to India in May 1964. He settled in Chandigarh with his wife, one daughter and two sons. At the time, his elder daughter was already married and settled in India. In February 1968 he flew to London, to arrive there just before the deadline for a new immigration bill, for a possible settlement but returned to India three months later, via Kenya. After educating and settling his seven children, he traveled regularly with his wife Angrez to England and the USA, to visit them and the grandchildren. After a short illness, Kartar passed away in Chandigarh on January 13, 1997, at the age of 84. Angrez continued to live with their daughter in Chandigarh, where she passed away peacefully in her own bed on July 13, 2009. She was 93.

Shangara Singh Sumal, younger brother.

After retiring from his job in Kenya in 1964, Shangara moved to Chandigarh in India, with his wife and two daughters. In February 1968 he flew to London with his brother Kartar, due to the same immigration bill. He lived with his son and worked for a short while as an electrician, before moving back to India. After the mid-1970s, he regularly traveled with his wife to London and America to spend time with their four children and grandchildren. He passed away peacefully in his sleep in Chandigarh, on June 4, 1994. He was eighty years old. After his death his wife Jaswant moved to New York to live with their daughter. She passed away on October 24, 2021, at the age of 99, ending the golden era of that generation.

Gurdial Singh Sumal, youngest brother.

He spent his entire life in the ancestral home in Lalheri village, and after the departure of his three elder brothers for Kenya, he looked after the family farm with help from Wazir. His wife Gurcharan died in the 1980s in the family home in the village. Gurdial spent his final years with his daughter, who had built a house on the farm in Lalheri village. Gurdial suffered from a stroke, before passing away on August 28th, 1997. He was eighty.

THE THREE BROTHERS OUTSIDE KARTAR'S HOUSE IN PANGANI,
KENYA BEFORE DEPARTING TO INDIA AFTER THEIR RETIREMENT
(FROM LEFT: GURMUKH, SHANGARA AND KARTAR), 1963.

SPOUSES OF THE THREE BROTHERS ENJOYING THEIR MEAL AFTER HAVING FED THE
THREE FAMILIES. THE CLASSIC EAST AFRICAN METAL TEAPOT, CALLED BARIKA CAN BE
SEEN AT THE FRONT (FROM LEFT, ANGREZ, GURBACHAN AND JASWANT).
SHANGARA'S KITCHEN, JUJA ROAD, NAIROBI, 1962

About the Authors

<u>Jaihind Sumal</u> was born and brought up in Nairobi, Kenya. After completing a Bachelor's degree in Mechanical Engineering from University of East Africa (now University of Nairobi) he moved to London, England in 1968. He spent a year at University of London (King's College) to do his Master's Degree in Internal Combustion Engineering and soon began work in an engine research laboratory. While working at the laboratory he completed

his Doctorate degree, again from University of London (King's College) in 1976. His work on the development of a unique automotive fuel injector at a company in England, led to an offer of a position at Bosch in Germany in 1980, to work on the development of fuel injection system components. In 1985 Bosch transferred him to their development center in Detroit, followed by another transfer in 1994 to Charleston, South Carolina, where he lives now. He is enjoying his retired life with his family and his grandchildren, Mila and Bodi, while pursuing his favorite hobby of working on cars and motorbikes, a hobby which started in his youth, in Kenya.

Inderpal Sumal was born and brought up in Nairobi, Kenya. He attended Park Road Primary School, City Park Primary School and the Duke of Gloucester School in Nairobi. He was an accomplished athlete and in high school won the Victor Ludorum trophy for the best athlete of the year at the annual school sports day. He joined the Royal Air Force (RAF) in 1966 and enjoyed the experiences of his postings to Cyprus, Wildenrath in Germany, Northern Ireland and Falkland Islands. He retired from the RAF as Flight Lieutenant in May 2005. He worked as a Crown Servant in London after his retirement from the RAF, until 2015. Her Majesty Queen Elizabeth II honored him with the member of the Order of the British Empire (MBE) award on February 16, 2012. Hockey has always been the passion of his life and he has participated in national and international tournaments, excelling in a sport he has loved all his life. In October 2022, he represented Wales Over 70s team at the World Masters Hockey World Cup played at the Olympic stadium in Tokyo. His team beat South Africa in finals to be crowned the World Champions in the over 70s age group. He is an avid reader and is referred to as a walking encyclopedia of historical events by his siblings. He is enjoying his retirement with his family and grandsons Sahib and Gurjot, while keeping himself fit with gardening, running and playing hockey.

Kawal Neni Dhillon, née Sumal, was born and brought up in Nairobi. In the absence of Government primary schools for non-white girls at the time, she attended Arya Girls Primary School, a privately run Hindu school. In 1964 she won a scholarship to Kenya High School, a prestigious institution which had just opened its doors to non-whites after Kenya's independence from the UK, on December 12, 1963. The only black African girl in the school was Jane Kenyatta, the daughter of Kenya's first President. The presence of the first five girls of color, two of whom were on scholarships, was not easily embraced by white students and teachers. She felt relieved to leave that school after attending just one term, when her parents decided to move to India in May 1964. She completed her MSc Hons Degree in Botany (Cytogenetics) in 1973, at Punjab University, Chandigarh, but never worked in that field. She got married in 1974 and moved to London. After bringing up her son and daughter, she worked in a managerial role for the British Civil Service. She retired in 2014 and now spends her time enjoying her hobbies of creative writing, gardening, walking, and most of all, being a grandmother to her three little rafikis Jaya, Ray and Lillie.

The authors can be contacted at: jsumalbk@gmail.com

Milton Keynes UK
Ingram Content Group UK Ltd.
UKHW051513021223
433429UK00015B/226/J

9 798822 910508